HOPE IN DESPAIR

STORIES OF COURAGE IN KASHMIR

SUNANDA NEHRU GANJU

Vitasta

Published by
Renu Kaul Verma
Vitasta Publishing Pvt Ltd
2/15, Ansari Road, Daryaganj
New Delhi - 110 002
info@vitastapublishing.com

ISBN 978-93-86473-72-1

First Edition 2019
MRP ₹450

Cover Amaranta Nehru
Layout by Vitasta Publishing Pvt Ltd
Printed by Vikas Computer and Printers

To my noble father, Pushkarnath,
and devoted mother, Shanta,
without whom I would not be...

How to weave a Kani shawl

Together we walked through the seasons
Without any reasons
We played and laughed
Awed
Watching the burnt rust chinars in autumn sun glow
Kangris kept us as warm as our hearts did in the snow
Celebrating our differences and similarities with all
Was it ever your Habba Khatoon or my Arnimal?
Did Lal Ded resonate more in your words than mine?
Our Gods never did sign
A treaty of duality
Picking up the broken threads and reconciling
With weft of love and warp of healing
Motifs of almonds and paisleys entwine in symmetry
Each distinct yet fused in one tapestry….

—Sunanda Nehru Ganju

Contents

Acknowledgements

I am deeply grateful to all the protagonists who placed their faith in me by allowing me to interview and publish their stories despite the hostile climate in the valley. In a state where positive initiatives seldom get reported, these stories are uplifting and invigorating and will inspire people in and outside the valley about the reconstruction work of peace and development happening in the valley. However small or insignificant their efforts might appear at present, these stars will be the future course correctors in Kashmir.

I am indebted to Dr Amit Wanchoo and Hasrat Gadda who introduced me to a whole lot of changemakers. Gadda ji filled the missing pieces of information and Renu Khanna (well-known development consultant and rights activist) patiently went through the manuscript and provided her valuable inputs while Kruti Dalal did an excellent job with the editing. I will be eternally grateful to them. Dr GN Muju's compilation of the articles written by his esteemed father, DN Muju, and other stalwarts of Kashmir has been a vital source of information on the history of early education in the state. Amaranta Nehru deserves a mention for her exquisite cover design and illustrations in the book. I am thankful to Sushil Pajnu and all the known and unknown Kashmiris for lending me their support and escorting me to the most inhospitable areas of the valley.

Most importantly, I am indebted to my mother and brother for supporting me and for preserving our only home in Kashmir and to my husband for his constant encouragement. As a Kashmiri Pandit, having a home allowed me to be at ease and helped me to interact with people and sense their palpable desire for peace and rapprochement.

—Sunanda Nehru Ganju

Vadodara, March 2019

Foreword

They say that if you are a Kashmiri, you may leave Kashmir but Kashmir can never be taken out of you. There is something that draws you back, sometimes physically, sometimes on an intellectual quest. Sunanda Nehru Ganju is also drawn by an intense curiosity; what made Kashmir shake off its feudal, educationally deprived past and emerge into modernity in the 20th century and open up to transforming possibilities. She goes on to trace the near death blow that terrorism struck on educational institutions and educators towards the end of that century of hope.

This book is a labour of love. The author has embarked upon a journey to chart the so far unmapped territory of the beginning and growth of modern education in Kashmir. She has worked hard—researching the role of pioneers, interviewing living players and collecting untold stories of courage and determination. It is to my knowledge, the first serious study of the subject from which lessons can be learnt.

Her sources are primary as well as secondary. It seems that she has won the trust of those whom she has interviewed—they seem to have been readily forthcoming to give substance to her argument.

In the final analysis, it is an unvarnished tale, plainly told, of path-breaking individuals and institutions, that gave education in Kashmir firm roots and showed by example how it could be an instrument of change, bring about awareness and empowerment and thus 'conscientise' the oppressed.

—Neerja Mattoo
Kashmiri educationist and writer
March 2019

Why this Compilation?

IN THE late eighties, the first separatists initiated a toxic combination of political and religious aspirations of people in the Kashmir valley. Suddenly, their radical ideology (self-determination and formation of Islamic state) took the most sinister and grotesque turn, shattering the deep faith and trust amongst communities of different faiths. Hindus (Pandits) were hounded out of the valley to never return to the land of their ancestors. They lost their roots and identity, and felt betrayed by their own people. Many years after 1990, a local Kashmiri Muslim aptly described a land eroded of its secular traditions: *Is it good to see the same type of flowers everywhere? A garden looks beautiful with variety of flowers and colour...*

With the rise of Islamic fundamentalism and separatist forces in the valley, there has been a complete breakdown of the secular and democratic fabric of the society. With the ousting of the Kashmiri Pandits (Hindus) from the valley, the state has lost its pluralistic character and true *Kashmiriyat*—a culture marked by a unique blend of Shaivism, Buddhism and Islamic Sufism which had led to a climate of peaceful coexistence for centuries.

Today, there has been a tremendous rise in literacy and educational attainment of young girls and boys (especially amongst the Muslims), but divisive and fundamentalist forces are gradually pervading and curbing their freedom of expression. This is visible in the introduction of hijab at a very early age and the move to prevent large number of women (barring some from elite sections of the society) from participating in mainstream development. Recent incidents such as the burning of 27 government schools (since July 9, 2016) points to the lowest and darkest period in the history of modern Kashmir. One news item comments, "*The separatists and the fundamentalists in the Kashmir Valley are determined to turn back the clock and take the Valley once again to the medieval era where the Maulvis and Qazis ruled the roost and their writ ran unchallenged.*" (Gupta, Ref 9)

Against these dismal and despairing conditions, I wanted to rekindle the legacy of the shared history of interfaith communities that absorbed multicultural and religious thought, which resulted in a Sufi tradition unique to Kashmir. Today, the fire of fundamentalism is at its peak and threatening to engulf other nations. As a Kashmiri, I wanted to draw attention to the great legacy of our land and give an opportunity for diversity, tolerance, secularism and freedom of expression, and above all humanity to survive. This is our last chance before it is too late.

Our Rich Legacy

Tomes have been written on the history of Kashmir time and again with differing perspectives of various writers who reflected the problems and political conflicts of their times and the era in which they lived. Kalhana's immortal work *Rajatarangini*, composed in 1148–49 CE is our oldest record of the kings and their dynasties. Kalhana relies upon traditional sources like *Nilmata Purana* (an ancient text written before the 8th century), inscriptions, coins, monuments, and his own personal observations. Thereafter, bearing the same legendary name *Rajatarangini*, the history of Kashmir has been written by three authors—Srivara, Pragyabhatta and Shuka, who wrote the history of their own eras. The last written one by Shuka chronicles events till Akbar's conquest of Kashmir in 1586 CE. King Zain–ul–Abidin of Kashmir has the credit of translating Kalhana's *Rajatarangini* into Persian in the 15th century.

As per Nehru PN (Ref 24), the history of Kashmir can be traced to 3450 BCE with Gonanda dynasty where people were Hindus with Hindu rulers. Somewhere in the middle of 4th century BCE, Buddhism entered Kashmir. Around 326 BCE, Alexander reached India and was welcomed by King Abhisaras, whose sway included parts of Kashmir as well. After his departure, the Greeks established chiefships in the regions extending to north–west India. Demetrious became king of a vast territory, including Kashmir, while Menander exercised sovereignty over Kashmir. The Kashmir valley became part of the empires of Ashoka and Kanishka who brought and nurtured Buddhism. At that time, Brahmins and Buddhist monks journeyed from the valley to the north and eastwards along the silk route, and carried the message of Buddhism to what are now parts of Afghanistan, Tibet and Mongolia. During this period, there was widespread

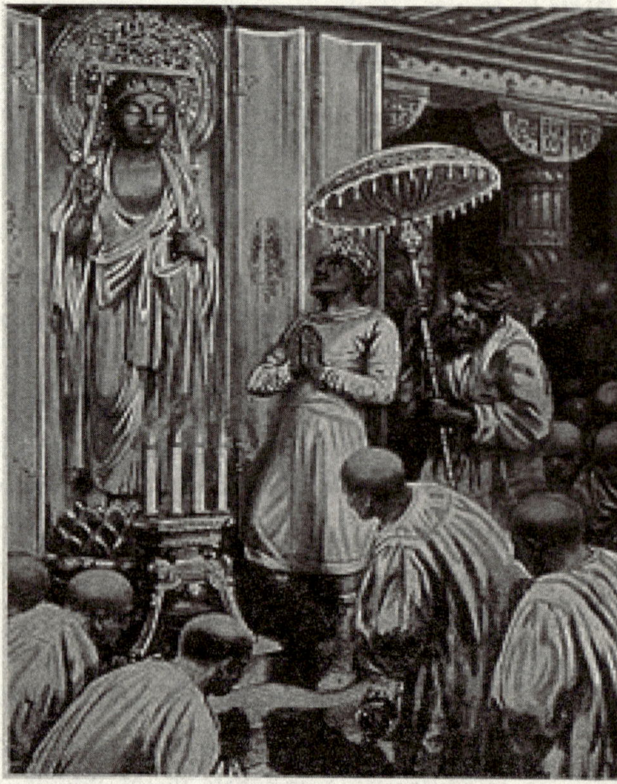

Kanishka inaugurates Mahayana Buddhism in Kashmir

conversion to Buddhism amongst the lower castes of Hindus and soon only the Brahmins were left.

The 6th to 8th century CE witnessed the decline of Buddhism in Kashmir and the restoration of *Nilmat* (Vedic and Shakti culture) followed by re-emergence of *Panchratra* (Vaishnava culture). Except for the political domination of the early Buddhists under state patronage of Ashoka, and later the Kushans, there was no religious strife. Mihirkula was the only persecutor of Buddhists, and he was part of the backlash against the religion throughout the subcontinent. Finally, Buddhism was totally wiped out in the country.

Hari Parbat is a symbol of multi-cultural and religious structures that surround it. The hill, which rises 122 metres from the valley floor, contains a temple revered for its image of the Goddess Sharika and shrine of Guru Chatti Padshahi. On the southern side is situated the shrine of Maqdom Sahib and the mosque and monastery of Akhun Malla Shah, the preceptor of Dara Shikoh, the eldest son of Shah-Jahan the great Moghul ruler.

Bakshi (Ref 3) observes that the elitist Brahmins regained their power and clout during the decline of Buddhism in the valley. The Brahmins excelled as scholars and made significant contributions in religious philosophy (Trika School of Kashmir Shaivism), Sanskrit and areas of medicine, history, art and architecture. This is the time when Kashmir came to be known

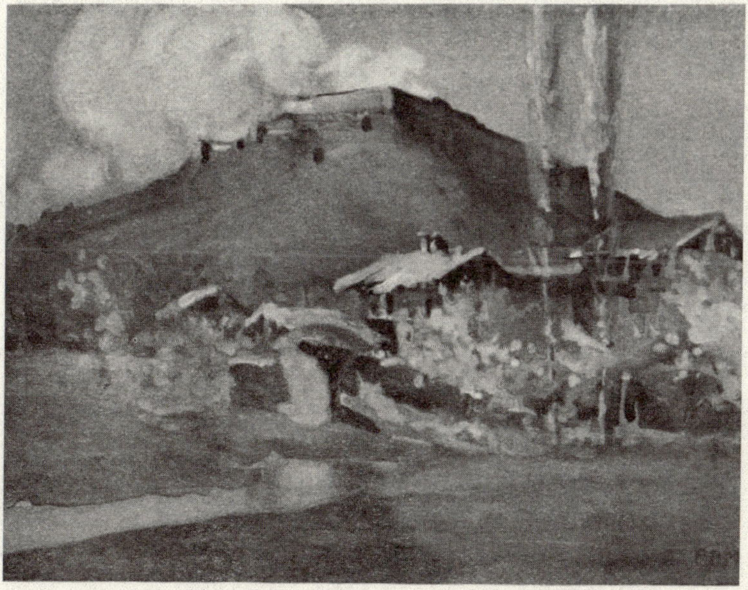

Hari Parbat

(From 'A Sketching tour in the valley of Kashmir' by Miss Patty A berigh-Mackay)

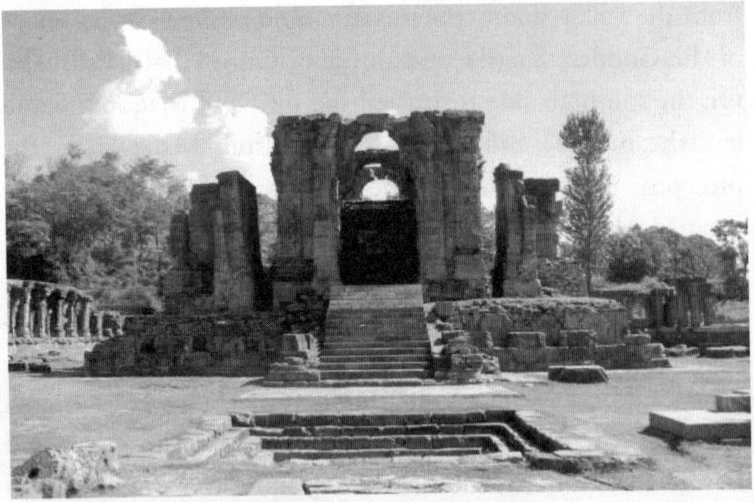

Martand Sun Temple Ruins today
(The Temple was built by the third ruler of the Karkota Dynasty, Lalitaditya Muktapida, in the 8th century CE)

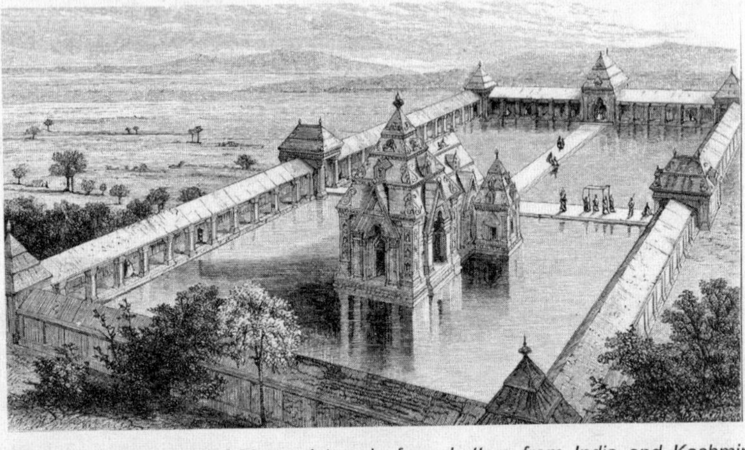

Restored impression of Martand temple from *Letters from India and Kashmir* by J Duguid (1870-73)

as Sharda Peeth—a seat of learning. The ruins of the temple of Sharda and the university are currently situated along the Neelam River in the village of Sharda, in the Pakistan-administered state of Azad Kashmir.

Bakshi mentions that:

> The rulers mercilessly exploited and suppressed the common people. However, there was no bar of caste or birth to a person who wished to hold civil or military positions. Both Brahmins and lower castes were appointed as soldiers and there was no restriction on inter-caste marriages. Laltaditya was the son of a king belonging to the Karkota dynasty, by a woman from the Vaishya community (trading class). Similarly, another warrior king, Shankarvarman's mother was the daughter of a low caste distiller. These reflect the lasting effects of Buddhism's classless and casteless society even until the 10th century CE. Another Kashmiri king married an untouchable Domba woman. As queen, she had entry into a Vishnu temple and her relatives were appointed as ministers.
>
> The ruling house of Kashmir formed alliances with India and the Turkish dynasty of Kabul, who were Buddhists and Hindus till one thousand CE. Kanishka, the Indo–Scythian ruler of Kashmir and the Turkish family of Kabul founded the Sahi dynasty whose territories extended till Punjab. The famous queen Didda was the granddaughter of a Sahi King. The last of the Sahi kings was defeated by a Muslim Turk, Mahmud Ghazni. After their defeat, Sahis took refuge in Kashmir and continued to hold positions of power and intermarried with the ruling class.

Thus, we note that before Islam spread from Central Asia to Kashmir, Kashmir already had diverse ethnicity and a syncretic religious and social culture.

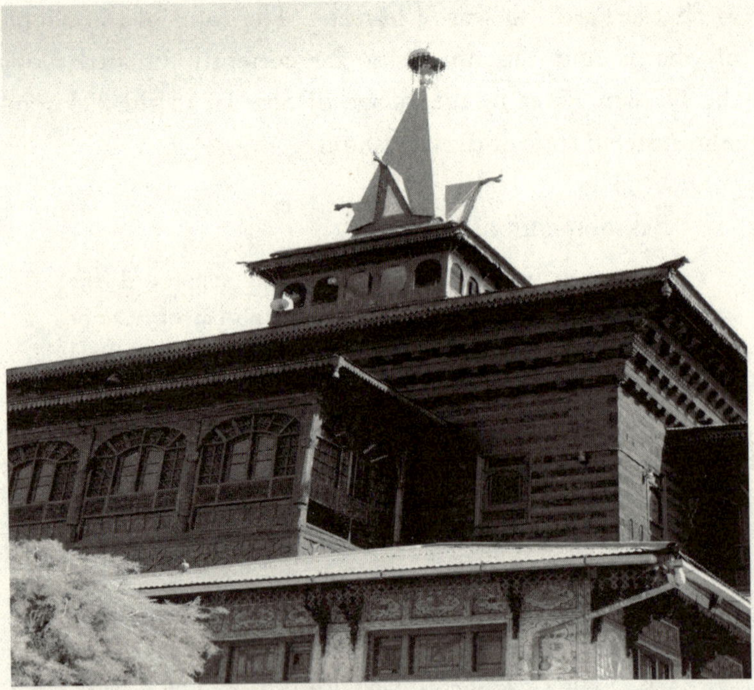

Shah Hamdan Mosque, Khanqah-i-Mu'ala

The Muslim rule in Kashmir was established in the 14th century, and continued till the beginning of the 19th century. The Sikhs and the Dogras ruled the state for over a century under the British crown as the sovereign power. Hence, Kashmir became a melting pot comprising Hindus, Buddhists, Muslims and Sikhs. Can we negate the fact that Kashmir has at least 5,000 years of history where Hindus, Buddhists and Muslims lived and spread important teachings and contributed in language, philosophy, astrology, and aesthetics in drama (natyashastra), arts and crafts? The first Islamic preachers came as Sufis teaching the basic tenets of Islam based on brotherhood and equality. Rulers who came from Central Asia helped people to acquire skills in crafts, embroidery, carpet weaving and paper maché for which their artisans were world-renowned. The territories under the Sikh rule (1819-1839) extended beyond the Jammu Region and the Kashmir Valley to the Tibetan–Buddhist kingdom of Ladakh and the emirates of Hunza, Gilgit and Nagar. After the Anglo-Sikh War in 1846, the British gave the title of 'Maharaja' to Gulab Singh as a reward for aligning with them against the Sikhs. Gulab Singh was made the ruler of Kashmir under the provisions of the infamous Treaty of Amritsar, whereby the British granted the state to Gulab Singh and his heirs for Rs 75 lakhs and helped him during his reign in Kashmir. Thus, with the advent of Sikh and Dogra rule, Kashmir was brought close to Jammu and then to Punjab.

With the legacy of a syncretic culture, can we forget the makers of modern Kashmir? Kashmiris will always remain indebted to Annie Besant, who set up educational institutions

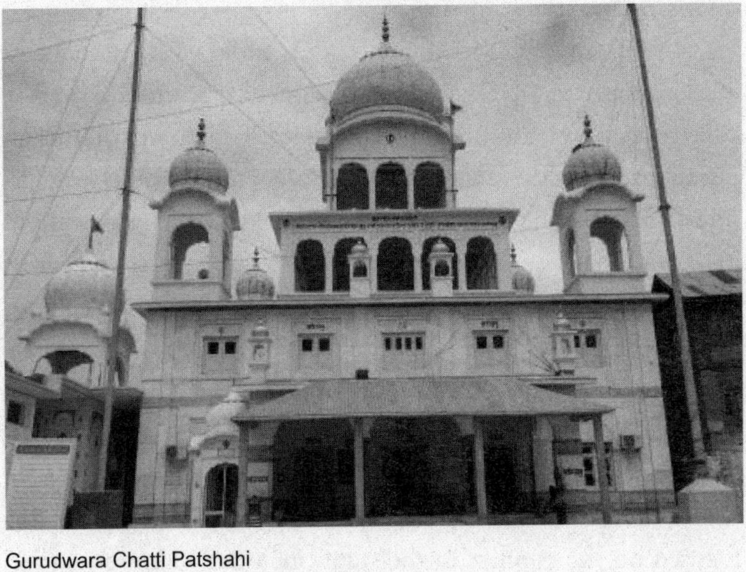

Gurudwara Chatti Patshahi

to emancipate people and help them break the shackles of oppression and religious bigotry, along with Christian missionaries who introduced modern education in the valley. From a *terra incognita* lost behind the mountains, they brought Kashmir to the forefront. Can we forget the first educationists who worked tirelessly for modern education, especially women's education? Can we forget social reformers like Kashyap Bandhu and Prof SK Toshkhani, who changed the status of women and worked for widow remarriage and child marriage in the Pandit community? Can we forget Hriday Nath Wanchoo, who toiled for the rights of the downtrodden in the state? Can we forget Maulvi Gulam Rasool Shah and women like Begum Akbar Jehan, Begum Zaffar Ali, Sajida Zameer and Mehmuda Ali who initiated an educational revolution amongst Muslim girls? Can we forget great leaders like Sheikh Mohammad Abdullah who helped abolish the zamindari system, ensured transfer of land to the tiller and fought for the uplift of the poor and disenfranchised?

Bakshi Gulam Mohammad and Sadiq were fathers of modern Kashmir who built medical, agricultural and engineering colleges; teacher training colleges, not to mention numerous primary and middle schools. Can we forget the men and women's militia (comprising Hindus and Muslims) who came forward to protect Kashmir against Pakistani tribals in 1947? Can we forget Habba Khatoon and Arnimal who brought elements of pathos and longing in Kashmiri language and poetry? Can we forget the *rishis* and saints like Lal Ded and Nund Rishi who have nurtured us for generations through their spiritual wisdom?

Everything changed after 1990. Numerous books have been written on the Kashmir cataclysm. Muslim writers focused on the conflict in the state (including excesses carried out by the Indian army on the locals) with a historical and political background. Kashmiri Pandits who were killed and hounded out of the valley, overtly and covertly, produced yet another set of writings on their exiled status and suffering. The question that intrigues me is: can we get any *amrit* (nectar) in this great *manthan* (churning) that could guide our children and the future generations? How do we reduce feelings of hatred and resentment between communities and restore the rich pluralistic character of our state?

As I searched for solutions to the Kashmir imbroglio, I started noticing how people were quietly and succinctly reconstructing, rebuilding and trying to salvage the broken pieces post 1990 despite the obstacles. It was like reviving a comatose person bit by bit with perseverance and dedication.

To understand the present state of degeneration, I needed to briefly highlight what the past was just a hundred years ago and how people from both communities have persevered and endured unimaginable hardships to bring Kashmir to the level it attained in the pre-nineties. History gives us a reference point to compare the present. Hence this compilation touches upon the contribution of educationists and social reformers who made Kashmir modern, free, and democratic and promised to uphold the rights of all communities in the late nineteenth and early twentieth centuries. It also traces the period of conflict and devastation in the 1990s. Within the backdrop of cross firing, sirens, curfews, shut downs and destruction emerge stories of brave men and women who withstood the era of militancy and continued to rebuild their state from ruins. For this reason, I have included people from education, politics, literature and arts, rehabilitative and development services as well as environment and sports. Some of the stories are so incredible that it is difficult to imagine how valiantly those people fought those battles and continue to do so even today. Others find it so painful to narrate that they prefer not to recall their stories. The interviews with the bravehearts and rebuilders have been carried out in April-May 2016 and May–June 2017, and are purely based on their ad-libbed responses with some information added from their past interviews and publications. Section 1 gives a historical perspective of the educational and social reforms; Section 2 provides a glimpse of the changing face of Kashmir post 1990, and Section 3 underscores the role of bravehearts and rebuilders in today's conflict-ridden Kashmir.

Section 1

Modern Education and Social Reforms

IN THE middle of the nineteenth century, there was a stir up and sounds of change were awakening the nation. The uprising against the British rule in India and the revolutions that were happening in Russia, China, Egypt, Ireland and Turkey, along with the theosophical movement and the work of the Christian missionaries were all paving the way for a new world. Kashmir, although geographically alienated behind the mountains, could no longer remain impervious to the changes in India. Ideas of freedom, liberty and equality were reverberating and echoing the world over and the ripple effect touched Kashmir through the homegrown social and religious reformist organisations like the Arya Samaj amongst the Pandits and the Anjumans spearheaded by the Mirwaiz and other maulvis amongst Muslims. A revolution was created by their cumulative impact.

It is in the bedrock of the Dogra regime that medical services, educational and social reforms took place due to cogency of the Christian missionaries, British Resident in the state, religious and social reformers and the Theosophical Society of India. Whether it was political ideology, health, sanitation, education or administration, there was a sea change in all spheres of life. Men and women could take advantage of western education that opened their minds and developed their intellect. Against this reality, when women were offered to break free through the various social movements in the state, it catapulted towards an age of renaissance for both men and women.

The Dogra rulers have been condemned for the gross exploitation of the agrarian population and denial of rights of the majority population resulting in the mass political and social uprising in the thirties and forties against the feudalism of a Hindu king ruling a Muslim majority state. However, when we look at the contribution of the Dogras to the state, one is humbled by their vision. Aside from education, the credit for opening much of the far-flung mountainous territory and arid Himalayan plateaus goes to the Dogras. During Maharaja Pratap Singh's reign (1885-1925), the valley was connected to the outside world by two major road networks—Jhelum Valley Cart Road from Kohala to Baramulla was completed in 1889 and Banihal Cart Road connecting Jammu to Srinagar was opened to public in 1922. Aside from opening schools and colleges, Maharaja Pratap Singh opened Amar Singh Technical Institute for fine arts and crafts way back in 1913. However, the institute was closed down later for reasons unknown. The process of modernisation was accelerated during Maharaja Hari Singh's rule (1925–1947) when he developed tourism and boosted infrastructure development. He also introduced the concept of Jabri schools (compulsory education). The status of several primary schools was raised to middle standard and the first high school was established in Srinagar under the auspices of Punjab University.

The sections below briefly describe the changes that took place towards the end of nineteenth century till the early fifties.

Improvement in Health

When the Christian missionaries arrived in the valley in 1864, the health condition of the masses was appalling. Poverty, poor hygiene and high morbidity and mortality rate, especially during epidemics, which broke out frequently, was a matter of grave concern. High maternal and infant mortality rates were a common feature as were child widows. At that time, there were no hospitals and people relied on *hakims* (traditional healers) to treat them. Prompted by the deplorable health conditions, the Christian Missionaries Society in London introduced modern medical services in the state. Suspecting the intentions of Christian missionaries to spread Christianity in the state, both Hindu and Muslim reactionaries thwarted the attempts to initiate medical services in the state. But Reverend Robert Clark, the first missionary, accompanied by his wife, started a dispensary for women, where the government subsequently opened the Diamond Jubilee Zenana Hospital. In 1865, the Christian Missionary Society allocated a substantial sum for the medical work. Dr Elmslie, a Scottish man of saintly nature, was deputed to found a hospital. At that time, no European was allowed to remain in the valley in winter. He took refuge under a Chinar tree to examine patients and to dispense medicines. He performed small operations in the open. Unable to get adequate accommodation the following year,

Dr Elmslie pitched a tent and used it for examining patients. During that season, he treated 3,365 sick men and women. As a direct impact of his efforts, the government started a first state dispensary at Srinagar in 1870, which proved to be the forerunner of the State Medical services. In 1874, Maharaja Ranbir Singh granted an ideal site on Rustom Gaddi Hill near Dalgate for the construction of the hospital. Two brothers, Dr Arthur Neve and Dr Earnest F Neve and their sister Ms Nora Neve (Superintendent of Nurses) performed stellar services at the hospital for more than two decades and earned the deep affection of the people for their selfless service (Bazaz Ref 4).

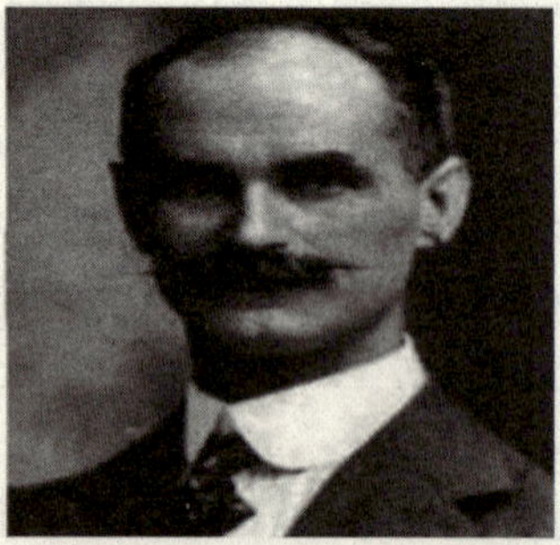

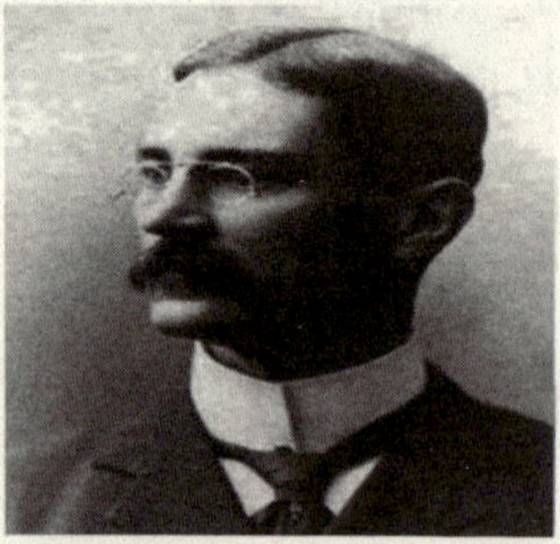

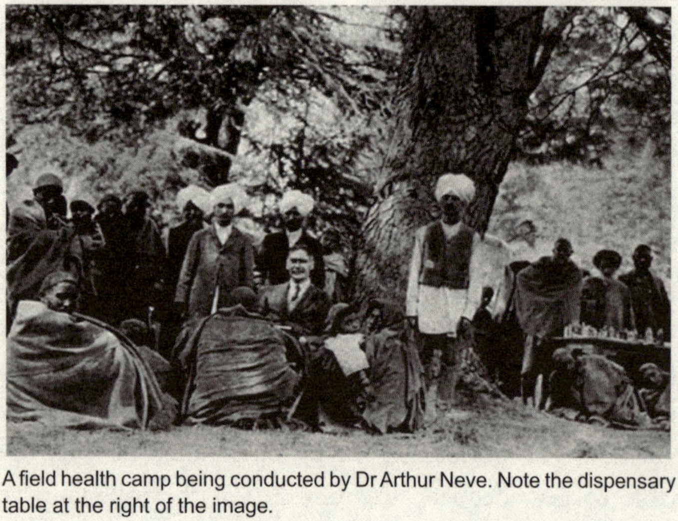

A field health camp being conducted by Dr Arthur Neve. Note the dispensary table at the right of the image.

In 1888 Dr Fanny Butler, the first woman medical missionary in India, started a dispensary in Srinagar city called the Zenana Shifa Khana under the aegis of the Church of England Zenana Missionary Society (CEZMS) at Rainawari. Another hospital was opened in Anantnag. Nursing activities were championed by the likes of the indefatigable Irene Petrie and Miss Robinson, as well as another woman, Miss Kate Knowles MB, who worked there in the beginning of the twentieth century. One Elizabeth Mary Newman was bestowed the title of the *Florence Nightingale of Kashmir* by Canon Tyndale-Biscoe for her work at the CEZMS Hospital. Prompt in responding to famines, floods and cholera, the missionaries influenced the government in taking steps to alleviate the suffering of people.

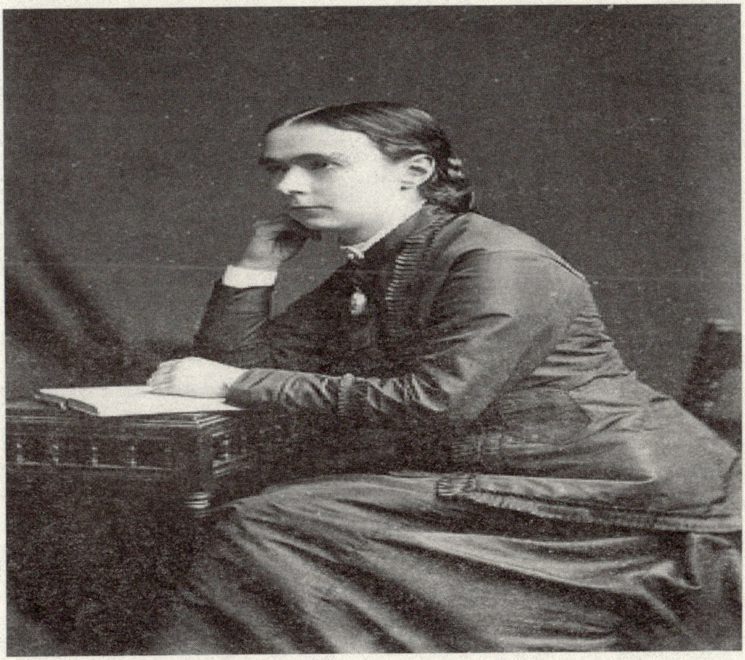

Fanny J Butler, Medical Missionary (Died in Kashmir, October 26, 1889)

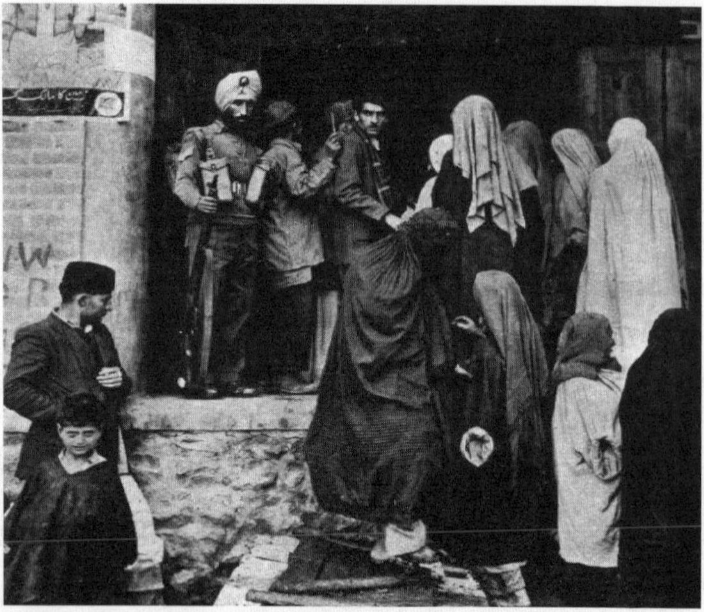

Women waiting at the dispensary (Early 1900s)

The foundation stone of the State Hospital (SMHS) was laid by the Marquess of Linlithgow, the Viceroy of India in 1940 at the estate of the Hadow Mills Carpet Factory. This is the reason why the hospital is known colloquially as *Hadwun* (Hadow's) Hospital even today. The first medical college in Jammu & Kashmir started functioning at Hazuri Bagh on the banks of the Jhelum at the site of the present *Lal Ded Hospital* in 1959. The Government Medical College Srinagar was inaugurated at its present-day location in Karan Nagar by Bakshi Ghulam Mohammed, Prime Minister of the State of Jammu and Kashmir, in 1961 (Jehangir, Ref 11).

The First Educational Institutions

During Muslim rule, the Persian language flourished in the valley due to the presence of Sadatas/Sayedds who came to

Kashmir from Central Asia for the purpose of proselytization. As a result, Persian became the court language. New *maktabs* (Arabic word for elementary school) and *pathshalas* (Hindi word for elementary school) were opened where Persian and Sanskrit were taught. However, education imparted in both Hindu and Muslim institutions continued to be religion-oriented. This is clearly visible in the writings of Tyndale Biscoe (1863-1949), a British missionary and an educationist who worked in Kashmir. In his book, *Kashmir in Sunlight and Shade* (1925), he observes: The indigenous schools of Kashmir have always been in connection with the mosques, where the boys are taught to read Arabic so that they may be able to read the Quran, but not necessarily to understand it. Likewise, the Brahmins have their schools, where Sanskrit is taught so that the boys may be able to read the sacred Hindu books.

Bakshi mentions that during Afghan rule, most old documents referring to land records were in Sharada script (an abugida writing system of the Brahmic family of scripts) developed before the 3rd century. It was used for writing Sanskrit and Kashmiri and needed to be translated to Persian. Thus, some Kashmiri Pandits discovered the value of learning Persian. Knowledge and skill in handling numbers and monetary transactions helped them find positions in the land revenue departments of the state. Astute minds and careful diplomacy helped them to find positions as advisors, *vazirs* to the foreign rulers whether Afghan, Sikh or Dogra.

Similarly, when the British were imposing their might in the state under the Dogras, the Pandits were the first to learn English as a language. Thus, they were quick to grab opportunities for their survival, as they were historically involved in learning and teaching like all Brahmins in the rest of the country. Initially, the fruits of modern education were reaped by the children of Kashmiri Pandits. The Christian Missionary School (CMS) was in fact monopolised by them. However, unlike their male counterparts, the Pandit women were barred from opportunities to seek knowledge and led a difficult life. On the other spectrum, majority of the Muslims did not show much interest in English education due to many reasons. Poverty and the clout of their clergymen (who suspected that western education would make them Christians), coupled with the lack of encouragement given by the ruling monarchy to educate Muslims further contributed in keeping them out of the formal education system.

Sikhs were another minority community whose status was similar to the Muslims and marked by low educational attainment and social backwardness. The chief Khalsa Dewan, the first socio-political organisation of Sikhs was formed on 30th October 1902. Their main objective apart from learning Sikh scriptures was to promote spiritual, intellectual, moral, social, educational and economic welfare of the Khalsa *panth*. The Khalsa Youngman's Association was established in 1917 and the Sikh Sahayak Sabha was established in 1920 with the same objective of spreading education and protecting the rights of Sikhs in the state. With the Khalsa and Sikh Sabha movement, Sikhs began to get conscious of their rights and also participated in the Akali Dal[3] movement initiated by the Sikhs in Punjab (Kaur, Ref 16).

3 The Akali movement, also called the Gurdwara Reform Movement, was a campaign to bring reform in the gurdwaras (the Sikh places of worship) in India during the early 1920s. The movement led to the introduction of the Sikh Gurdwara Bill in 1925, which placed all the historical Sikh shrines in India under the control of Shiromani Gurdwara Parbandhak Committee (SGPC).

Impact of Theosophical Society on Education

History is witness to how a tiny seed of thought can change the course of events and lead to an impact across nations for centuries to come. Whether it is the French, Russian or Chinese revolution, people have always welcomed an alternative to their oppressed condition.

Muju GK, (Ref 22) in his compilation *Drops of Nectar* traces the contribution of a Russian woman, Helena Petrovna Blavatsky (1831-1891) who dared to challenge the triumph of material sciences and racial superiority and proclaim boldly the truth of the Universal Brotherhood of Humanity, without distinction of race, creed, sex, caste or colour. With the help of HS Olcott (1832-1907), Blavatsky founded the Theosophical Society on 17th November 1875 at New York during a time when racial discrimination was practised even in advanced nations like the United States.

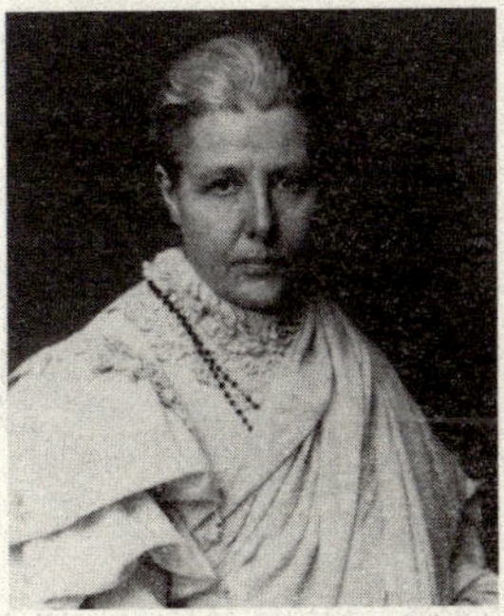

Dr Annie Besant (1847-1933) did some remarkable work in the country under the auspices of The Theosophical Society of India. The Society was the first international organisation in modern times which included Europeans, Asians and Africans, men and women, white and coloured as members on equal footing. The winds of this movement swept into Kashmir also where a branch of the society was established in 1900 as Kashyapa Lodge in Srinagar by some prominent people like Vas Kak Dhar, Ved Lal Zutshi, Anand Kaul and others. According to Dayakrishen Muju (educationist and member of The Theosophical Society of India), Maharaja Pratap Singh (1885-1925), was operating on the instructions of the British residents of Kashmir. He did not allow colleges to be set up and was opposed to higher education for the Kashmiris. Tyndale Biscoe, the principal of the CMS School, was supposed to do pioneering work in education in Kashmir, but he invariably discouraged his students from joining college. Teaching in his schools (besides games) never attained a high standard, except in English, which was necessary for producing clerks and reading the Bible.

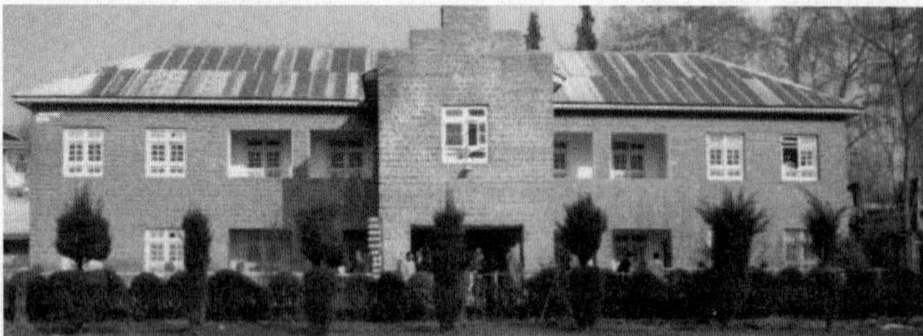

Sri Pratap Higher Secondary School

Two schools were opened in Jammu and Srinagar in 1874—Ranbir High School, Jammu, and Srinagar Middle School, Fateh Kadal. With the advent of Sri Pratap Singh in 1885, modern education in the state took concrete shape and continued to expand. In 1891, the school was raised to Srinagar High School and was later was called Sri Pratap High School.

As per Muju, Annie Besant of the Theosophical Society approached Maharaja Pratap Singh and requested him to donate a piece of land so that a new building could be constructed for the school's future growth. Initially, the Maharaja did not agree and Besant tabled the issue in the British parliament, pressurising the Maharaja to donate land in Kothi Bagh area. Thus, a new building for a college was built there with the liberal donations of Kashmiri Pandits. This college later became known as Sri Pratap Hindu College.

Prior to the college, there was no provision for higher education in the valley. Acquiring higher education outside the state was not only expensive but also cumbersome, as students had to undertake long journeys to reach Lucknow or Allahabad and arranging accommodation was a difficult proposition.

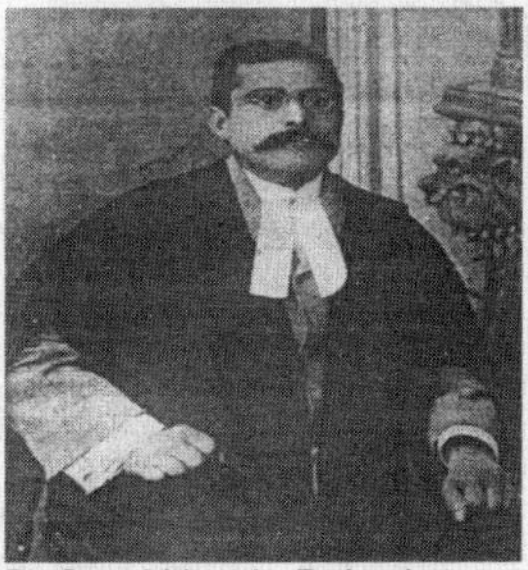
Pt Suraj Narain Bahadur

In the beginning, Kashmiri Pandit boys used to stay in an area called Kashmiri Mohalla in Lucknow. Majority of the boys used to read Urdu or Persian (the language of the courts) in *maktabs* as it would fetch them good jobs. La Martiniere College was started in 1845, and was affiliated with Cambridge University, London. Progressive Kashmiri boys like Sheo Narain Bahar and Pran Nath Bazaz joined the college against the wishes of community members, for better career prospects. In 1864, Canning College was established in Lucknow. Pandit Sheo Narain Bahar joined the college and started a magazine called *Mursula-e-Kashmir* in 1872. Through his magazine, he tried to encourage young boys to acquire an English education. Thus, such enlightened members formed a club in Kashmiri Mohalla to carry out their ideology and bring in certain social reforms. Annie Besant appointed Pandit Suraj Narain Bahadur, a sub-judge and a great educationist, as the secretary of the Theosophical Society of India. She used to organise regular meetings of the society at his residence in Kashmiri Mohalla, Lucknow. The main thrust in the meetings would be education of Kashmiri boys and social reforms in the community.

Thus, Sri Pratap Hindu College formally started functioning as an intermediate college in 1905 and was formally inaugurated by Maharaja Pratap Singh in 1911.

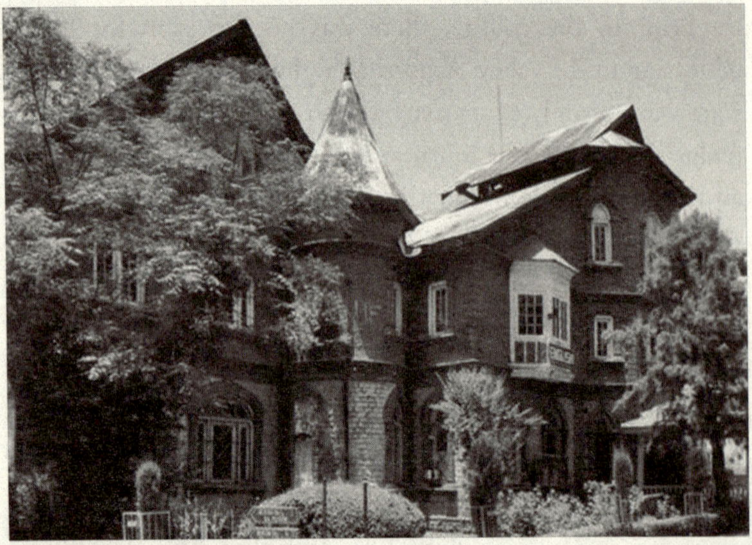

Sri Pratap Singh College

The British Government was alarmed to see the growing influence of Annie Besant in the valley. The then secretary of state wrote a note observing that "Mrs Besant's influence is bound to have political consequences and her religious teachings certainly tend and I believe are deliberately meant to promote the idea of an Indian nation, which is spreading gradually, and which, in course of time, may assume a form adverse to the British rule". This fear led the British Residence in J&K to ask the Maharaja to take over the management of the college. In July 1912, the Sri Pratap Hindu College was rechristened to a more secular Sri Pratap College and was affiliated to the Punjab University in Lahore. The board of Trustees of the Central Hindu College, Varanasi, authorised Dr Annie Besant to hand over the college to the government of Jammu and Kashmir on receipt of Rs 20,000 in consideration of the cost of the building and furniture erected and supplied by them.

Due to an unexpected increase in the number of students, the bifurcation of the college into Sri Pratap Intermediate College and Amar Singh Degree College was carried out on September1,1942. The first principal of Amar Singh college was Deen Muhammad Taseer. With the enactment of The Jammu and Kashmir University Act, 1948, all affiliations with Punjab University were withdrawn and in the same year, the two colleges were affiliated to the newly founded Kashmir University (Muju).

Rise of Christian Missionary Schools

CMS School: At first, the missionaries thought it prudent to administer medical relief to the people of Srinagar during the periods of epidemics. Their useful services encouraged them to fight illiteracy. In 1880, the founder Rev JH Knowles laid the foundation of the CMS (Church Mission Society) School on the hospital premises (Modern Chest Disease Hospital, Drugjan) in Srinagar. The school was started with five pupils. In 1883, the number of boys in the school increased to thirty. It was in 1890 that the government permitted the CMS to shift the school downtown and it was moved from the hospital premises (Drugjan) to Nawakadal, in the house of one Master Abdul Rehman which was situated on the banks of River Jhelum. As a result of this, the number of students increased to about 200 in 1890. Times changed, so that when Canon CE Tyndale-Biscoe joined the school in 1891, there were 250 pupils on the roll. The Primary School grew into a Middle School and eventually into a High School. In 1937, the CMS High School was shifted to Sheikh Bagh. It was renamed Hadow Memorial School after Major Hadow, a well-known carpet manufacturer and philanthropist who gifted this piece of land to the school. Later in 1946, the school was finally named after Tyndale

Biscoe. Biscoe is often credited with founding the modern education system in Kashmir, through western modernisation and rejection of local tradition.

In 1905, the Mill Hill missionaries set up St Joseph's School in Baramulla, and in 1942, Burn Hall School was opened in Srinagar.

The Girls Mission School was founded in October 1912 by Miss Violet B Fitze as the Girls' Mission High School in a mud house at Fateh Kadal. In the beginning, Miss Fitze had to face opposition from various quarters, but her calm confidence and perseverance bore fruit. By 1918, the school was raised to the middle standard and it received a grant of Rs 700/- from the Education Department of the State. Miss Fitze died in 1929. With the arrival of Miss Mallinson in October 1922, the school's name was changed to Mallinson Girls' School heralding a new age of educational and cultural advancement among the women of Srinagar.

Presentation Convent was started on 17th of March, 1936, but in the beginning the students were mostly British children residing in Srinagar and had European teachers. Later, local students were also granted admission and it became a girls' only school (sourced from the school websites).

Role of Women's Welfare Trust (WWT)

Women's Welfare Trust was formed in 1926. As mentioned above, it was a formidable task to open educational institutions for boys, but to deal with the education of girls was, in Kashmiri parlance, as difficult as *gaenti thool vaalun* (to get hold of kite's eggs). Except for a few *maktabs* where only religious education was imparted, there was no arrangement for girls to be educated. Muju remarks that it was the Theosophical

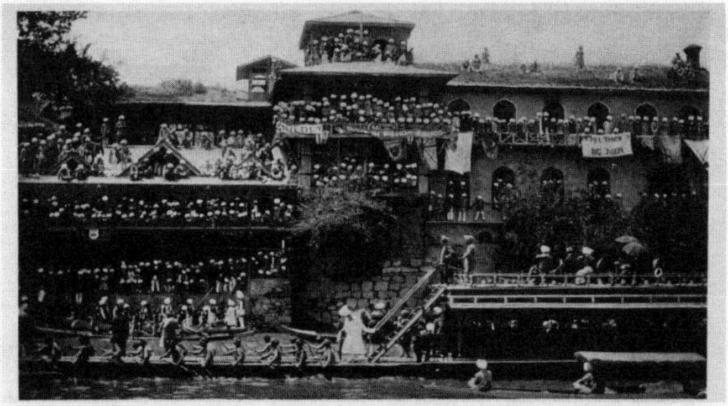

THE CHURCH MISSION SCHOOL WELCOMING HIS HIGHNESS

This unique mission school of the Church of England is a potent factor in the upbuilding of Kashmir. It is held in high esteem by both the people and the ruler. Here each year a royal welcome is accorded the Maharaja on his return to his palace at Srinagar.

theory that regarded women as equal to men, which prompted a band of youthful theosophists like SK Toshkhani and Aftab Kaul Nizamat (details given below) to garner public opinion by asking *"How can you regenerate the home life of Kashmir, raise the society from sloth and backwardness and rid it of ignorance and superstition?"* The unanimous response was that women should be educated. Thus began the birth of Women's Welfare Trust in 1925, the Golden Jubilee Year of The Theosophical Society. The formation of the Trust was, however, sanctioned by the state government in 1926. In September 1926, Women's Welfare Trust was launched with an objective to "advance the welfare of the Kashmiri women by imparting to them knowledge, by stimulating home industry among them and by promoting their physical health and wellbeing". The founding members of the Trust were Ms Margaret Cousins, Ms LD Van Gheel Gildemeester, Aftab Kaul Nizamat, Shrikanth Toshkhani and Shridhar Kaul Dulloo.

Pandit Aftab Kaul Nizamat was born in 1886 and educated in CMS High School. Although a topper in his school, he did

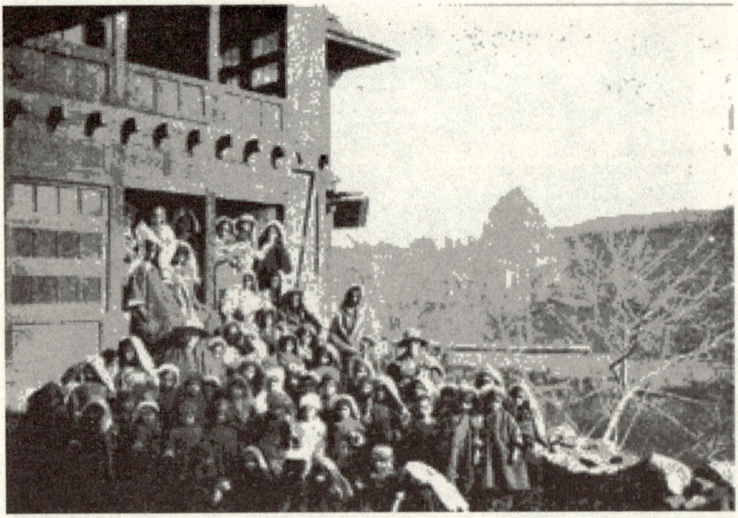

Miss Fitzes' School

not pursue his studies beyond matriculation.His father had died young. Aftab Kaul served as a subordinate official in the Audit Department of the Kashmir government. He would provide books and soaps to the needy students of the school run by the trust. He also launched a campaign among poor students to encourage regular bathing and maintaing personal hygiene. Mrs Devki Kaul (Aftab Kaul's wife), also took a leading part in regeneration of the community in 1931-34 and organised demonstrations in support of social reform. Bazaz pays a moving tribute to Aftab Kaul. He says, "I can say that among the builders of modern Kashmir who are not much known but who are entitled to the gratitude of posterity, Aftab Kaul Nizamat is surely one. If ever we decide to construct a temple of fame for the illustrious sons and daughters who lived and died for the welfare of humanity and freedom of the Kashmiris, this noble soul should have a niche reserved for him in it."

Prof Shrikanth Kaul Toshkhani was a linguist, educationist, social reformer and thinker—an outstanding personality of Kashmir endowed with extraordinary intellectual and moral qualities. Prof Toshkhani got his preliminary education at a *maktab* run by an Akhun Sahib in Khanqah-i-Mohalla, Srinagar, where he learnt some Persian. He graduated from SP College, obtained his Master's degree in Philosophy from Allahabad University and followed it up with an LLB from Agra University. He mastered half a dozen languages including Sanskrit, Pali and Prakrit. He started his professional career as a lawyer in Anantnag and later joined SP College and Amar Singh College, Srinagar, as a Professor of philosophy, logic and psychology.

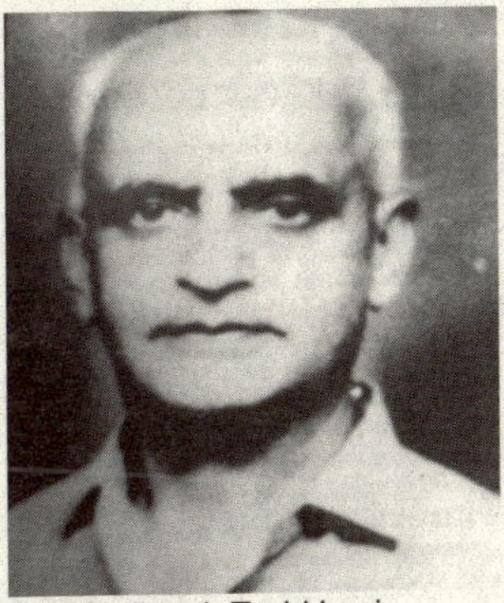
Prof Shrikanth Toshkhani

Prof Toshkhani was one of the torchbearers of women's rights in Kashmir that had snowballed into a movement for women's education. As a founding member of Women's Welfare Trust (WWT), he wrote textbooks in Kashmiri on all subjects, including geography and arithmetic, using modified Devnagari script so that women could be taught in their own mother tongue. At that time, the government did not even recognise Kashmiri as a dialect. In the initial stages, he also trained teachers in teaching methods and proved to be a man ahead of his times. He wanted to draw public attention to the despicable plight of women by using written and film media. He wrote his first novel in Kashmiri in 1923, at a time when Kashmiri prose was non-existent. Titled *Leela*, the novel was serialised in

Bahar-e-Kashmir, a trilingual community magazine published from Lahore. What is significant is that it highlighted the struggle of Kashmiri women against outmoded social practices that degraded them and suppressed their individuality. However, little is known about this book. Dr SS Toshkhani in his article in *Unmesh*, January-March 2000, observes that this book has hardly been mentioned because it was written in Devanagri script.

Later, Toshkhani produced and directed his first film in 1927 on issues like widow remarriage but the film could not be released because the conservatives (which formed the majority) opposed it vehemently and resorted to heavy stoning to prevent the movie from being screened. GEC Weikfield, (who served in the government of Jammu and Kashmir and was Prime Minister between 1929 and 1931) was compelled to withdraw it. Toshkhani was appointed by the J&K Cultural Academy as the Chief Editor for Kashmiri and Kashmiri–Urdu dictionaries owing to his profound knowledge of lexicography. He represented the Kashmiri language at various forums in the country (Muju).

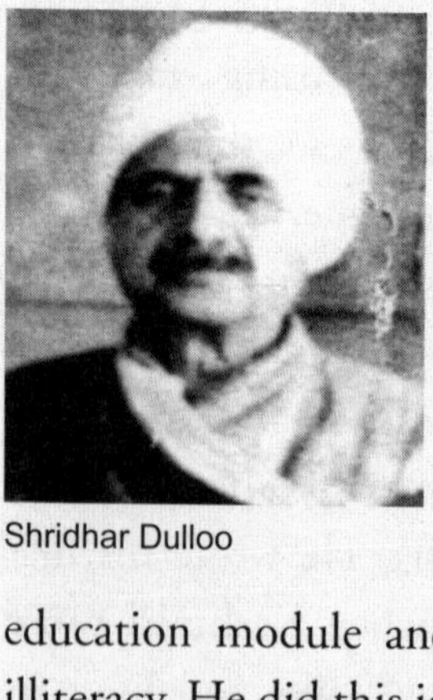

Shridhar Dulloo

In every meeting held by the WWT team, Shridhar Joo Kaul Dulloo (1892-1967) would always say that they had kept the area of Ladakh in total darkness. His burning desire to move to Ladakh became a reality in 1939 when the Maharaja transferred him to Ladakh as an Education Officer with clear directions to start the basic education module and pull Ladakh out of the darkness of illiteracy. He did this job with utmost dedication and devotion till 1948. In fact, he is responsible for sending Ladakhis to schools and enlightening generations. He also authored a book *Ladakh through the Ages* that had a substantial impact on the social and political awakening of Ladakhis and led to the formation ofThe Buddhist Association. Impacted by Buddhist culture and the message of Buddha, Dulloo eventually became a Buddhist (Mota, Ref 21).

There were other shining members also who contributed immensely towards women's education but due to the limitations of this compilation, I have not been able to elaborate their role in the activities of the Trust. What was unique about the Trust was its policy of giving membership to only those who followed a secular and a nonpartisan ideology.

The first school founded by this trust was the Vasanta (the Indian name given to Annie Besant) Girls High School. The school could only muster five girls at first. It was opened at Kral Khud, Srinagar, in the house of Pandit Shivji Bhat, a Brahmin priest, who became the first teacher at the school. Out of the five students, one was his own daughter. The noble Brahmin never asked for any remuneration for his work. It was only when the school began to grow and donations were collected that he accepted Rs 7 as his monthly allowance. With this small beginning, the ardent workers continued their efforts for women's uplift through education. More schools were opened in Drabbiyar, one at Bhorikadal, one at Badiyar and another at Rainawari.

Even though the schools were run by The Theosophical Society, the Muslims did not favour sending their girls to school. The theosophists struck a novel idea. One Maulvi Hamza Shah was running a private *maktaba* at Kral Khud, Srinagar in the vicinity where Pandit Aftab Kaul Nizamat lived. The maulvi was making a little earning by receiving small customary gifts from his students. Through persuasion and tact, combined with an offer of a regular and a fixed salary, the theosophists were able to convince him to transfer his *maktaba* to the Women's Welfare Trust. The school was named Muslim Girls School, Kral Khud, and the maulvi became its de facto Head Master. While the maulvi continued to teach the Holy *Quran* and other religious scriptures as usual, the school was given a teacher who could teach Urdu, Arithmetic, Geography and Hygiene. Another teacher was appointed to teach handicrafts. With their first success, efforts were made in other places as well. Maulvi Sar-ud-Din who was running a *maktaba* at Kalashpora, in the vicinity where Prof Toshkhani lived, also followed suit. The school was

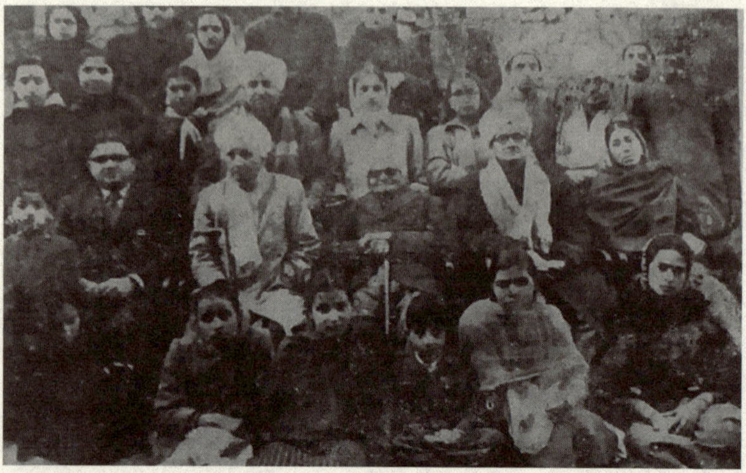

Master Zinda Kaul[2], Shankar Kaul[3] and others at Kashyapa Girls School (source: internet)

2 Master Zinda Kaul(1884–1965) was a well-known Kashmiri poet, writer and teacher. He composed in Persian, Hindi, Urdu and Kashmiri. Kaul also translated works of Kashmiri into English, Persian and Devnagari.

3 Shankar Kaul joined CMS school Fateh Kadal in 1892 as a student and later rose to become Head master of this school. He is also known for his exemplary social service.

named Mohammadan Girls School and a third *maktaba* run by Maulvi Nizam-u-Din Akamali was taken over and named Islamia Girls School. Soon these schools were made middle schools. Khemlata Wakhloo, a noted politician reports that the teachers at Vasanta School would go to homes of girls who would attend *maktabas* for religious teaching, and ask them to come to schools and learn languages, science and social studies.

The government sanctioned liberal grants for the Trust. In 1939, the Vasanta Girls School became a high school and the first batch of girls appeared for Matriculation examination under Punjab University, Lahore. Muslim girls started seeking admission in higher classes in Vasanta High School. By then, the trust was running eleven schools. In 1951, the state government decided to stop grant aid to private agencies and took over the management of the schools under the trust. Thus, the trust had to curtail and consolidate its activities. The only two schools that remained under the trust were Vasanta Girls High School at Nai Sadak, and Kashyapa Girls High School at Chhota Bazar, Srinagar (Muju).

Post 1990, there was total devastation and the two schools were greatly damaged. With supreme efforts of the trustees like TN Ganju and Dr GK Muju, the schools are still running and serving the lower income sections of the society. Pandit Dina Nath Muju (father of Dr GK Muju) was also a lifelong member of the Women's Welfare Trust, Kashmir, who worked for the emancipation of women and their education. He was mercilessly killed by terrorists in 1990.

As per Bazaz, in the early years the trust employed only Hindu teachers for Hindu schools and Muslims for Muslim schools. Due to the paucity of Muslim teachers (who were allured by better salaries of government jobs), Hindu men were taken as teachers in Muslim middle schools as early as 1931. Apprehending resentment from the parents, the trust members were pleasantly surprised to see parents congratulating the teachers for having introduced the change. Whenever there are communal tensions, there is a trust deficit between the two communities and so it was in 1931 as well. Nonetheless, the Pandit teachers continued to work unwaveringly at their posts.

In the summer of 1930, encouraged by the popularity of the girls' school, an Adult School was opened with three young women, Sidha Lakshmi, Posha Kujji and Radha Mal, in Pandit Aftab Kaul Nizamat's house. Bazaz notes that these women were openly ridiculed and discouraged by society. People felt that this initiative would be a failure, but after only four months, the number of students increased to fifteen. Most of the women were widows in their twenties; some had babies in their arms, while two or three were elderly women with grown up children. As applications poured in for more admissions, the school was shifted to a rented house in the vicinity and was called Seva Sadan. There were 32 women on the rolls in 1931. Seva Sadan also became a hub for not just the poor and destitute but also for common women who aspired to become independent. The syllabus of the school included handicrafts and tailoring apart from the three Rs (reading, writing and arithmetic). Many Seva Sadan students were recruited in government schools and other private teaching institutions. The trust also sponsored a Women's League with the objective of holding debates and discussions on social evils, unhealthy customs, causes of prevalent diseases, role of patriotic women in the reform movement and ways to achieve all round progress. Ranim Ded Razdan was the President and Devki Kaul (wife of Aftab Kaul) was the Secretary of the League.

Government Initiatives for Women's Education

Despite facing stiff opposition, the state authorities managed to open a primary school for Hindu girls at Fateh Kadal in the heart of the city. Two brothers, Hargopal Kaul and Jankinath Kaul, both spirited lawyers, voluntarily cooperated with the educational officers to open the school. A Kashmiri Pandit woman became the first teacher. She volunteered to work in the school despite the taunts and jibes directed towards her and taught there till the early 1920s. She was a familiar figure in Srinagar and was known as *Tekri Master*. Hargopal's daughter, Padmavati (affectionately called Nanni), became a widow when she was a child and remarriage was disallowed. She was educated privately. Defying the hostile public opinion, the liberal father offered the services of the bold girl as a teacher of the school, which later was shifted to Chinkral Mohalla and upgraded to middle level. Padmavati served the school till her retirement. The school was popularly known as Nanni's Chathhal School and it was here that the first batch of girls received their lessons in the three Rs, besides instruction in handicrafts like tailoring and embroidery.

In course of time, the government eventually started a Muslim school for girls with an advisory committee of liberal Muslims to look after it. The difficulties encountered by Muslim educationists were no less formidable than those confronted by Hindus. The medium of instruction in Hindu schools was Hindi in Devnagri script and in Muslim schools it was Urdu in Persian script. During that period, Kashmiri was yet to be recognised as a language by the state. By 1920, apparently girls' education had registered some progress. Besides the three mission schools, a new non-denominational high school was run directly by the State Education department; a Muslim school and five Hindu schools (three of middle level) were functioning in different parts of the city. 'However, not a single matriculate came out of these schools and the number who passed Middle Level Examination was also not large' (Bazaz).

Maharaja Hari Singh also founded The Kashmiri Women's Welfare Association in 1927 after a meeting was convened with Weikfield who formed the central organisation to coordinate and extend the work done by the association under the patronage of the Maharaja. The Women's Welfare Trust (founded by the Theosophical Society of India) became a part of the Kashmir Women's Welfare Association and undertook many educational and income-generating projects. Maharaja Hari Singh built a purdah garden where women assembled, relaxed, held meetings and picnics, celebrated festivals and young girls and children played games. He opened a separate department for women's education. Since qualified teachers were unavailable locally, he recruited teachers from Punjab, UP and even Bengal.

Higher Education for Girls

In 1931, Sri Pratap College was the only institution where university education was imparted to students of the Valley. Although there was no ban on girls to join the college, they were reluctant to join the all boys' college (500 were enrolled) after matriculation. In a bold move, Vimla Kaul, wife of social reformer Kashyap Bandhu, who had qualified for the university course before her marriage, applied for admission in the spring of 1932. This created a stir in the college, but fearing public criticism, the government relented and provided all facilities to the young woman to secure admission. Bazaz says, "It was a strange spectacle to find a solitary woman moving amongst hundreds of young men or sitting in a classroom side by side with them." Vimla had to undergo many trials, but she persevered till the end and became a role model for several young women who started enrolling themselves in the college. Her boldness and quiet dignity encouraged many hesitant girls. She was the first Kashmiri woman who went to UK to secure an MEd degree. On her return, she was promoted to the post of Inspector of Schools. Another woman who did commendable work is Begum Zaffar Ali, who worked as the Chief Inspector assisted by two other inspectors, Uma Razdan (Srinagar division) and Khurshid Begum (Baramulla division). In 1946, the first batch of two girls who qualified as doctors from two Indian universities included Dr Krishna Dhar and Dr Prabha Labroo. Dr Jagat Mohini (wife of Dr Omkarnath Thussu) also gave her untiring services to the poor classes in Srinagar.

Vimla Kaul was the first woman to study in all boys' Sri Pratap College in the early thirties However, Bazaz remarks that he felt dejected that Muslim girls were lagging behind in education and parents were unwilling to send them to colleges. In 1944, he expressed this concern strongly in the columns of *Hamdard* (the first weekly newspaper in Urdu published by PN Bazaz and Sheikh Mohammad Abdullah) and many young Muslims agreed that it was the need of the times. In their published letters, these young Muslims strongly advocated co-education and made appeals to parents to send their daughters to local colleges. In 1943-44, 32 girls (from both communities) were enrolled in SP College. By 1947, half a dozen Muslim girls were studying in the colleges. The opening of the first Government College for Women in 1950 provided an emancipated forum for the women of Kashmir, furnishing

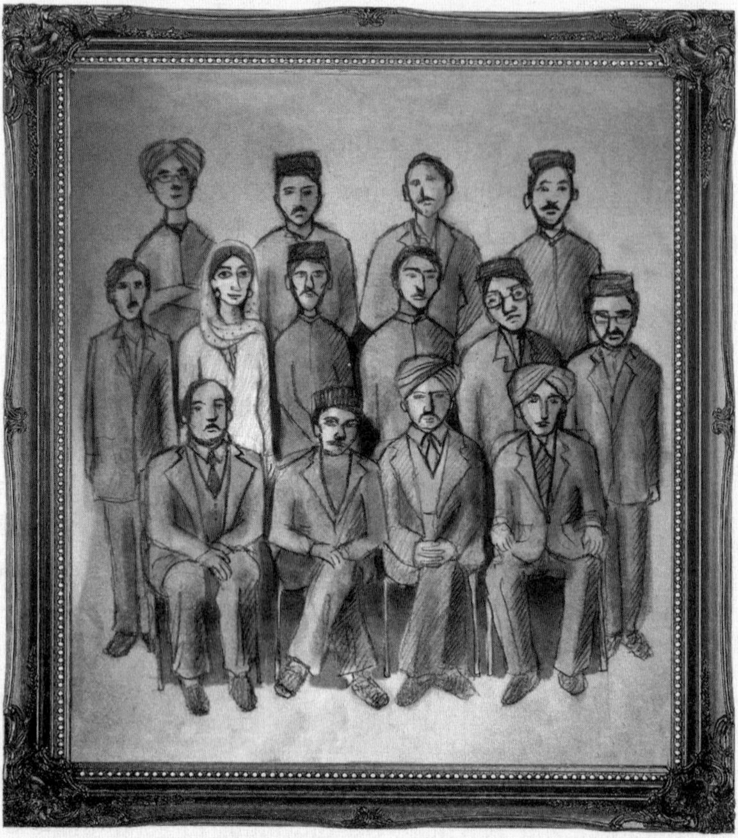

And she stood solitary, tall and resolute.

an instrument of change as more and more women joined the college. Thus, we note that the winds of change were having a sizeable impact on Pandit as well as Muslim women, who were also coming into the fold of newfound freedom and were able to breathe freely, to get educated, to express themselves fearlessly and to develop their intellect.

Parimoo (Ref 26) says that the Kashmiri Pandits, whose educational background was almost hereditary, were instrumental in introducing the Kashmiri Muslims to the light of modern education by slow but sustained efforts. They stood by Maulvi Rasool Shah in undertaking the pioneering work in Muslim education despite the warnings of the dire consequences if they continued to meddle in the religious affairs of Muslims. It is worth mentioning that the Islamia School was established with the active support of Kashmiri Pandits. Manned by Pandit teachers of high academic worth, the school has been a fountainhead of the educated elite of the Kashmiri Muslim Society.

Social-Religious and Educational Renaissance amongst Muslims (1899-1950)

The Mirwaiz of Kashmir: Parimoo describes how the religious institution of Mirwaiz is unique to Kashmir and has played an important role in the politics of Kashmir owing to the great admiration and respect people of Kashmir have for the religious seat of authority. He says, "The institution is nearly six hundred years old and evolved after Syed Ali Hamdani and Sheikh Nooruddin Sheikh (Nund Rishi) made a strong spiritual impact on the masses." The Mirwaiz, besides being a religious leader, also holds a position of a senior advisor to the Muslim Community. It was Maulvi Rasool Shah (born on 3rd September 1855) who, on becoming the head priest or Mirwaiz of Srinagar, awakened the Muslims educationally and, with the passage of time, became responsible for the changes that Muslims felt in their social life as well. In 1899, he founded an organisation called Anjuman-e-Nusrat-ul-Islam (ANI) and set up a network of schools throughout Kashmir, enabling thousands to receive education. These schools mainly taught Arabic, Persian and Urdu. ANI later opened Islamia High School despite opposition from conservative sections.

According to Peer (Ref 28), the Islamia School educated

the Muslims of Kashmir for three generations. It appears that initially when the school was started, there was not enough money for the buildings, so people kept earthen bins in their houses and put in a handful of rice every day. Shopkeepers kept collection boxes and asked every customer to donate an anna (a sixteenth part of a rupee). Every month this rice and money was collected. The rice was sold and the proceeds kept for building the school. That was the time when the people lived in abject poverty and suffered excessive taxation from Maharaja Hari Singh and his revenue officials. Hasrat Gadda (well-known writer and promoter of literary and cultural conclaves in Kashmir) informs me that Maharaja of Baroda constructed a building for Islamia School in 1940. In 1961, the government of Jammu and Kashmir established the autonomous educational institute of Islamia College of Science and Commerce during the tenure of Late Bakshi Ghulam Mohammad, the then Chief Minister of the state.

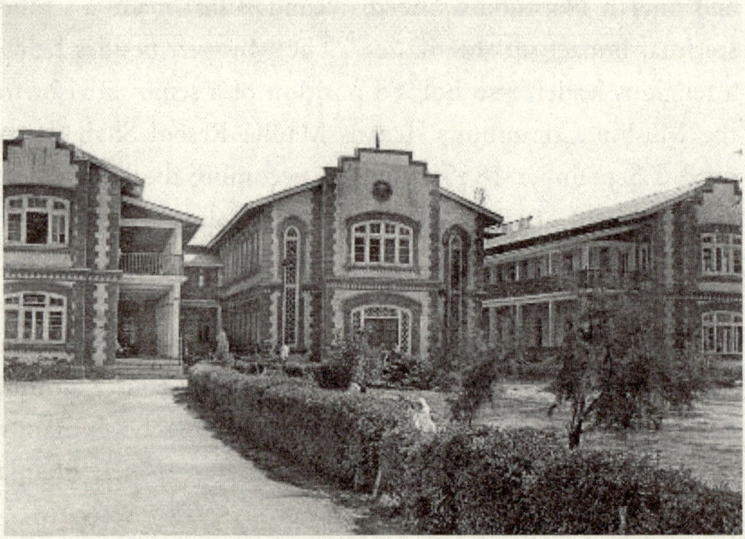

Islamia School

Sources from the internet claim that ANI also extended its domain in the field of social reforms. The aim of launching reform movements in the Muslim community was to save extravagant expenditure on marriage ceremonies and other functions like circumcisions, etc. including sending *Khabras* (paying a courtesy call to the bride and taking gifts in cash or kind to the daughter's in-laws).

With the establishment of the British residency in the early years of the twentieth century, the Muslim petitioners put forth their demands in 1908, highlighting the educational backwardness of Muslims and their abysmally small proportion in the state services. They complained of religious persecution and undue exploitation by their Hindu fellow citizens. Muslim zamindars were entitled to limited farm produce and lived in abject poverty. They resented the fact that all the high offices were taken by Punjabi Hindus and considered it unfair. It was not just the Muslims but poorer classes amongst Hindus were also in a dire state.

It was during this period that a Muslim Kashmir Conference was held at Lahore in 1911. In 1912 and 1913, the Muslim Kashmiri Conference condemned the preferential treatment of non-state subjects. In 1915, at the All India Muslim Educational Conference, a memorandum was presented to Maharaja Pratap Singh that demanded educational facilities for Muslims and a greater representation in the state services. Thereafter, a number of Muslim organisations mushroomed from 1918 onwards like *Anjuman-i-Taraqqi-wa-Ittihad, Anjuman-i-Taraqqi Talim-wa-Ittihad* that mainly aimed for the advancement of education and providing scholarships to deserving Muslim students. *Anjuman-i-Hamdard Islam* was founded by Babu Mohammad Ibrahim and some Punjabi Muslims in 1914 and in 1915.

Anjuman-i-Islamia was founded in Jammu which for the first time proposed to open a school for girls in Srinagar but the project was shelved due to unavailability of educated Hindu or Muslim female teachers (Kaur, Ref 16). A school known as Islamia Hanfia Middle School was started in 1922 in Anantnag.

Kaur further observes that *Anjuman-i-Tahaffuz-i-Namaz-wa-satar-i-Masturat,* started in 1923, advocated for stopping trafficking of women and the registration of marriages in the court of law, apart from its emphasis on the learning of religious scriptures. In 1930, another organisation called *Anjuman-i-Islat-ul-Muslimin* also initiated social reforms and later transformed into a political outfit. It is under this organisation that in 1930, Muslim students of Sri Pratap College, Srinagar, submitted their demands to the Maharaja that mainly highlighted low educational attainment amongst Muslims, improvement of hygiene and cleanliness, dress, diet and standard of living.

However, the obscurantists and orthodox Muslims opposed all efforts for establishing new kinds of school for Muslims. Those who challenged the Mulla dictates were forced to abandon their plans for radicalising and reforming the mindset of the Muslim community. Despite all opposition, the die had been cast to herald a revolution that changed the course of history in Kashmir. There are countless men and women who have made a remarkable contribution to Muslim education.I have illustrated some prominent change makers who made an extraordinary impact on the political, educational and social life of common men and women during the early to mid-twentieth century.

Sheikh Mohammed Abdullah (5 December 1905-1908 September 1982) played a central role in the politics of Jammu and Kashmir. He was born in Soura, a village on the outskirts of

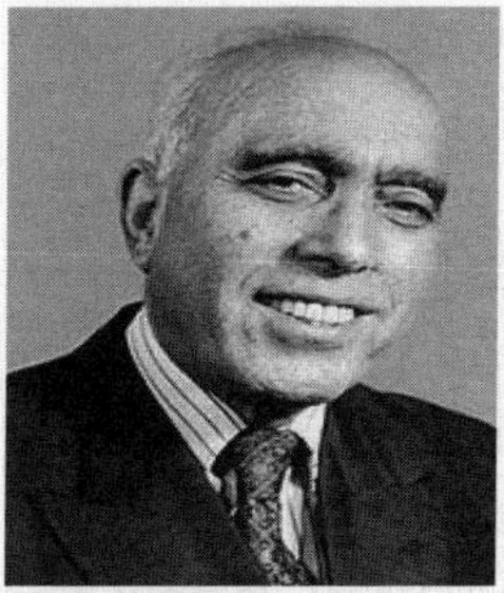
Sheikh Md Abdullah

Srinagar, eleven days after the death of his father Sheikh Mohammed Ibrahim. As per Abdullah's autobiography, *Atish-e-Chinar*, his father was a middle class manufacturer and trader of Kashmiri shawls. He was a descendent of a Kashmiri Pandit named Ragho Ram Kaul, who was converted to Islam in 1722 by the saint Rashid Balkhi. He graduated from Islamia College, Lahore, and obtained an MSc in Chemistry from Aligarh Muslim University. As a student at Aligarh Muslim University, he came in contact with and was influenced by persons with liberal and progressive ideas. He was convinced that the feudal system was responsible for the miseries of Kashmiris and like all progressive nations of the world, Kashmir too should have a democratically elected government.

During the reign of the first Dogra ruler Gulab Singh, positions in the administrative services were taken over by a number of Punjabis—the dewans of Emanbad were advisors to the Maharaja. Jwala Sahai, the first of such advisors, brought waves of Punjabi settlers to Kashmir, who were given extensive grants of land and positions of trust and power. Kashmiri Muslims and Pandits were relegated to the background. Pandits were eased out of offices, except for land record offices and village schools. Some fiefdoms (*jagirs*) were given to the Pandits.

Opposing this gross injustice, Sheikh Abdullah, Maulvi Abdul Rahi and Ghulam Nabi Gilkar were the first three educated Kashmiri youth to be arrested during the public agitation of 1931 against the Maharaja's repressive policies against the Muslims who formed the majority of the population in the valley.

Abdullah was popularly known as *Sher-e-Kashmir* (Lion of Kashmir), and was the founding leader of the National Conference. He served thrice as the head of government in Kashmir. He agitated against the rule of Maharaja Hari Singh and urged self-rule in Kashmir.

He was the prime minister of the state of Jammu and Kashmir after its accession to India in 1947 and was later jailed and exiled. He was dismissed from the position of prime minister on 8 August 1953 and Bakshi Ghulam Mohammad was appointed as the new prime minister. Sheikh Abdullah again became the chief minister of the state following the 1974 Indira-Sheikh accord and remained in the top slot till his death on 8 September 1982.

Sheikh Abdullah was the harbinger of national consciousness and instrument to introduce political mobilisation in the state. The three most significant goals enunciated in the manifesto *Naya Kashmir*, geared to the interest of the state agriculturists were the abolition of landlordism, land to the tiller, and co-operative association.

The Big Landed Estates Abolition Act, 1950, placed a ceiling on land ownership at 186 kanals (about 22 acres). The rest of the land of a landlord was redistributed among sharecroppers and landless labourers, without any compensation to the landlord. Transferring land without compensation was possible since the provisions of the Indian Constitution did not yet apply in the state. Conservative sections of the country's leadership had ensured that the right to property was included among the fundamental rights, which could not be challenged.

In May 1946, Sheikh Abdullah launched the Quit Kashmir

agitation against Maharaja Hari Singh. He was arrested and sentenced to three years imprisonment but was released only sixteen months later on 29 September 1947.

With the attack of the *Kabalis* from Pakistan in October 1947, Maharaja Hari Singh appealed to Lord Mountbatten, the Governor-General of India, for Indian military aid. The Instrument of Accession was signed on 26 October 1947. With the support of Mahatma Gandhi and Prime Minister Jawaharlal Nehru, Sheikh Abdullah was appointed as Head of the emergency administration by the Maharaja.

He raised a force of local Kashmiri volunteers to patrol Srinagar and take control of administration after the flight of the Maharaja along with his family and Prime Minister, Meher Chand Mahajan, to Jammu even before the Indian troops had landed in 1947. This group of volunteers would serve as the nucleus for the subsequent formation of Jammu and Kashmir Militia. Sheikh Abdullah took oath as prime minister of Kashmir on 17 March 1948.

On 8 August 1953, Sheikh Abdullah was dismissed as prime minister by the then Sadr-i-Riyasat (Constitutional Head of State) Dr Karan Singh, son of the erstwhile Maharaja Hari Singh, on the charge that he had lost the confidence of his cabinet (not the house). He was denied the opportunity to prove his majority on the floor of the house and his dissident cabinet minister Bakshi Ghulam Mohammed was appointed prime minister. Sheikh Abdullah was immediately arrested. He was later jailed for eleven years and accused of conspiracy against the State in the infamous 'Kashmir Conspiracy Case'.

On 8 April 1964, the State Government dropped all charges in the 'Kashmir Conspiracy Case'. Sheikh Abdullah was released and returned to Srinagar where the people of the valley accorded him an unprecedented welcome. After Nehru's death in 1964, Sheikh Abdullah was interned from 1965 to 1968 and exiled from Kashmir in 1971 for 18 months.

In 1974, he started talks with Prime Minister Indira Gandhi for normalising the situation in the region and they signed an accord called the 1974 Indira-Sheikh Accord. According to this, the demand for a plebiscite was given up in lieu of the people being given the right to self-rule by a democratically elected government (as envisaged under article 370 of the Constitution of India) rather than the puppet government, which had ruled the state till then.

Sheikh Abdullah assumed the position of Chief Minister of Jammu and Kashmir and remained so till his death in 1982. After his death, his eldest son Dr Farooq Abdullah was elected as the chief minister of the state .The transformation of rural Kashmir, as a result of his "sweeping land reforms", had far-reaching political consequences. Hundreds of thousands of newly empowered families would henceforth regard Sheikh Abdullah, seen as a principal agent of this transformation, as a messiah, and he earned the name Bab (father) among the rural masses. These peasant masses tirelessly backed Abdullah throughout his period of political wilderness after his dismissal in 1953 (Devadas, Ref 8).

Begum Akbar Jehan was married to Sheikh Abdullah in April 1933. She was the daughter of Harry Neadou (an Austrian who had married a Muslim Gujjar girl from Tangmarg and converted to Islam) who was part-proprietor of the well-known Hotel Nedous at Srinagar and Gulmarg. Their home was a queer mixture of western culture and Islamic traditions. At the age of 17, Begum Akbar Jehan passed the Senior Cambridge examination with distinction. For several years after her

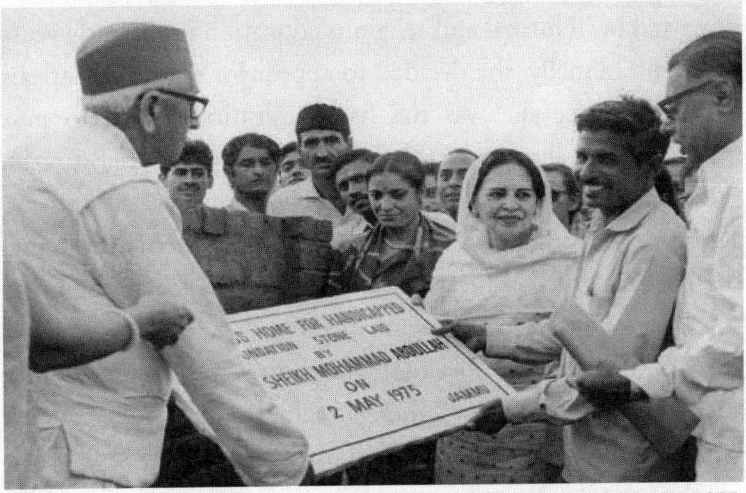

Begum Akbar Jehan inaugurating a home for the handicapped at Jammu in 1975

marriage with Sheikh Abdullah, she did not venture out in the public eye. After her husband and his colleagues were arrested in May 1946 for rebelling against the tyrannical rule of the Maharaja of Kashmir, she broke the shackles by removing her veil and joined the ranks of freedom fighters. She opened Madr-i-Meherban Welfare Centre, a centre for underprivileged and Gujjar women in 1974 in Miskeen Bagh and Ganderbal. Since her death in 2000, her daughter, Professor Surya Ali, is running the two centres

Begum Zaffar Ali (1900–1999), known as Syyeda Fatima Hussain, was the daughter of Khan Bahadur Aga Syed Hussain, the first matriculate of Kashmir, later Governor, Judge of the First High Court of Jammu and Kashmir, and Home and Judicial Minister during the Maharaja's rule. Syyeda Fatima, as she was known before her marriage, was brought up in an aristocratic, highly conservative Islamic setting where purdah was an essential part of a woman's life. However, the family believed in the importance of women's education and hence imparted both formal and religious education in the early years of her life. Finally, she decided to appear for the examinations in 1930. Since she was the first Kashmiri woman to pass matriculation, she was awarded the Gold Medal for her success. From then on, there was no looking back. She became a strong advocate of women's education and empowerment and joined the department of education as a full-fledged teacher. During this time, she started getting involved in social service, wherein she would provide clothes to the poor girls of the school, comb their hair, stitch their clothes, and look after their hygiene. Through the good offices of her father, grants were sanctioned for the schools. An extra sum of ten rupees was sanctioned for the maintenance of girls every month besides meals.

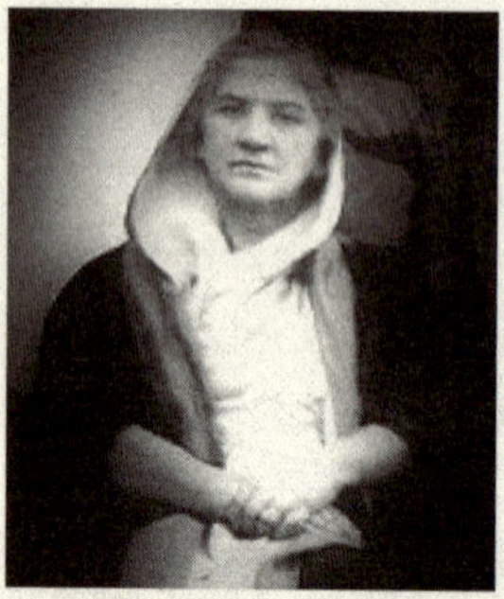

Begum Zaffar Ali

By 1938, Begum Zaffar Ali had completed her graduation and was receiving the requisite training in post-graduation courses. She served as the head mistress of various schools in different districts of the valley. She would go door-to-door convincing people of the merits of girls' education. Begum Zaffar Ali was later appointed as Inspector of Schools in Kashmir and became a source of inspiration for many girls who followed her footsteps. She served in various capacities in the department of Education—as a principal of various schools, Education Officer, Chief Education Officer and Chief Inspector of Schools in Kashmir. She also introduced mid-day meals in schools. During the later years of her career, she was appointed as Deputy Director, Education, and Director, Women's Education J&K. She was also a member of the Social Welfare Advisory Board, Jammu and

Kashmir. In the capacity of Deputy Chairman of the Advisory Board, Begum Zaffar Ali established a centre for technical training for illiterate girls in Chattabal area of Srinagar. She was also the Secretary of All India Women's Conference before 1947. Later, she became a Member of the Legislative Assembly (1977-1982) and played an important role in bringing reforms in education, women emancipation and other social issues.

In 1987, Begum Zaffar Ali was awarded the Padma Shri, the fourth highest civilian award in the Republic of India for her outstanding contribution in the field of social work. Later, she went on Doordarshan to return the award in protest against the neglectful and harsh policies of the government. She died in 1999 at the age of 99 at the residence of her son Agha Shaukat Ali in the United States of America (Wikipedia, n.d.).

Beginning of the Golden Age—1950s onwards

With the establishment of Government College for Women, the first women's college, on Maulana Azad Road, Srinagar in 1950, higher education among Kashmiri women started

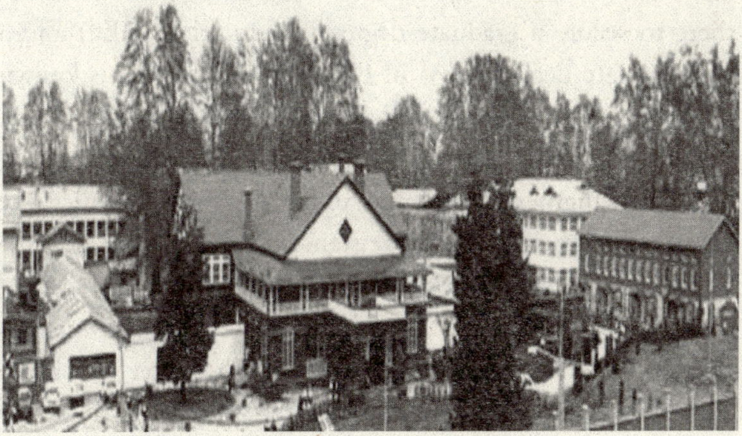

Womens College, MA Road, Srinagar

to gain popularity. In 1961, another college (Nawa Kadal College) exclusively for women was established and there was a huge change in the attitude of women and a rise in their consciousness. Some of the great educationists who left an indelible mark in the area of education in general and women's education in particular deserve a mention.

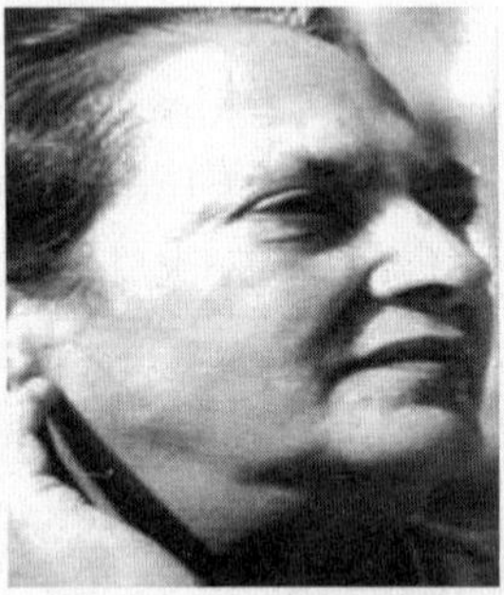
Mehmuda Ahmed Ali Shah

Mehmuda Ahmed Ali Shah was part of the then lone Missionary Girls School in Kashmir, now called Mallinson Girls School. Originally from Teetwaal, Karnah, her father Syed Ahmed Ali Shah had moved from his birthplace many years before getting married. Mehmuda had three brothers who would later become high ranking officials: Naseer Ahmed, a medical academic and a medical college principal, Syed Ahmad Shah, a Deputy Inspector General of Police and the third, Zameer Ahmad, a Sessions Judge. Moving to Lahore for her higher studies, she graduated in Arts (BA) from Punjab University, Lahore, and continued there to secure a graduate degree in Education (BEd) and a postgraduate degree (MA) in Political Science. She is known to be the first woman postgraduate of Punjab University, Lahore. She also did a postgraduate diploma course in Leeds, UK. Knowing her background and interest in academics, the Muslim Society in Punjab, Pakistan, offered her a job after she completed her masters. Some years later, the Maharaja opened up a school in Baramulla where Mehmuda was appointed as the headmistress. She served there till 1954, after which she shifted to Srinagar and was appointed the principal of the Government Women's College, MA Road.

During her tenure as the headmistress, and later as the principal, she is known to have worked hard to persuade the local women to pursue education. She also fought for the establishment of a second women's college and promoted arts and sports activities in the college. In 1975, she resigned from the college and reportedly influenced by her association with Indira Gandhi, moved to Delhi to get involved with the activities of the Indian National Congress. She served the party as a Secretary of the All India Congress Committee (AICC), but returned to Srinagar after Indira Gandhi's death in 1984, though she remained a member of the AICC. She also served as a member of the Jammu and Kashmir Legislative Assembly from 1987 to 1990.The Government of India awarded her the civilian honour of the Padma Shri in 2006.

In 2012, her alma mater, Mallinson Girls School, honoured her as the Most Outstanding Student of the Century. Mehmuda remained unmarried throughout her life. She died on 11 March 2014, at the age of 94, at her residence in Srinagar (Wikepedia, n.d.). After Mehmuda's death in 2014, Urmila Sharma, retired Principal, Govt College of Education, Jammu while paying tributes to her commented that she was a woman of secular ideas who used to love all students alike. She devoted her whole life to the cause of women's emancipation in Kashmir.

During her tenure, a weeklong drama festival would stage plays in English, Hindi, Urdu, Punjabi and Kashmiri. It was due to her initiative that an opera written by Dina Nath Nadim called *Bombur Ta Yemberzal* (Bumble bee and Narcissus) was performed and got appreciation from all quarters; similarly, a shadow play was also presented in the college auditorium. She also staged plays of Late Noor Mohammad Roshan in Kashmiri language.

Another leading and impactful personality was Professor Shamla Mufti born November 23, 1928. She completed her MA in Persian from Aligarh Muslim University (AMU) in 1955. She was a noted educationist, social worker and playwright. She was the principal of Nawakadal College, Srinagar and later Government College for Women. She inspired thousands of girls towards education and empowerment. She wrote a number of Kashmiri plays which were staged in the college and also published three books in Kashmiri.

Courageous, determined and brilliant are poor adjectives to define Krishna Misri (nee Zadoo) born in 1933 and brought up in Srinagar. Krishna rose to the post of principal, initially at Nawakadal College in 1975 and later took over as a principal at Women's College, Maulana Azad Road. As per Bakshi, Krishna's father, Vasu Dev Zadoo was among the early Kashmiri Pandits who went abroad to the USA for his civil engineering degree and training and returned with distinction to work in the state. He had three daughters and one son. His eldest daughter, Kamala was one of the first Kashmiri Pandit girls to graduate from the all-male Sri Pratap College. Zadoo needs to be credited with allowing his daughters to study in Sri Pratap College at a time when Kashmiri girls were largely confined to their homes. Most importantly, he permitted his daughters to join the Women's Self Defence Corps, the women's wing of the National Militia, organised by the National Conference in the wake of the onslaught on Kashmir by the tribesmen (*Kabalis*) from across the newly created border with Pakistan. The sisters lost their brother, Pushkar Nath, who defended the city against *Kabalis* before the first Indian troops were flown in to beat back the raiders following Maharaja Hari Singh's signing of the Instrument for Accession of Jammu and Kashmir to India in 1947.

As a member of the Kashmir branch of All India Women's Conference, Krishna was also associated with their major projects in the valley, such as the Dastakaar Anjuman and the Women's Cooperative in Miskeen Bagh, which trained women to become self-reliant by acquiring skills for production and marketing of handicrafts.

It is a pity that a family whose members sacrificed their lives for Kashmir and Krishna, who served the state as an educationist for decades, had to bid adieu to her home by divisive and fundamentalist forces in the nineties. She and her husband, Professor Mohan Lal Misri, of the Economics Department (University of Kashmir) were forced under dire threats to leave Srinagar at short notice. She now divides her time between Delhi and Abu Dhabi.

Originally known as Begum Rehana Jalal-ud-din (1913–2002), Barkat Begum came from a reputed family of Keran in north Kashmir, now synonymous with infiltration bids and covert military operations. Her father was a forest lessee, a big business during the Maharaja's time, and the family regarded education as a religious obligation. It was this sense which saw her siblings progress in their professions. Among her brothers and sisters, Nazir Ahmed Shah was a senior judge, Begum Me'raj Qureshi an educationist, Syed Ahmed Shah, aka Shamji, a founding member of the JAKLI Regiment, Dr Syed Naseer Ahmed Shah, a noted physician who won the 1984 Padma Shri for his services in the field of medicine, Syed Zameer Ahmed, a member of the armed forces and an entrepreneur, and Dr Mehmuda Ali Shah, a famous educationist.

Barkat was married to Agha Jalal-ud-din, an officer in Maharaja Hari Singh's Forestry Department, at a very young age but continued her schooling with her husband's support.

Later, in the 1950s, she boarded a steamer and travelled alone to Chicago to pursue a scholarship, leaving seven young children in the care of her relatives. It is said that her American sojourn triggered much speculation in Kashmir as she was one of the very few Kashmiri Muslim women to pursue studies abroad. She topped the list on graduating from Chicago University and also became the first Asian to score a hundred percent marks in her Master's degree. Her stay in the West took a heavy toll on her children who often had to go without meals. That ordeal, however, ended when she returned home with flying colours.

Thereafter, she dedicated her life to developing school education in Jammu and Kashmir, refusing to accompany her husband back to Lahore after Partition. She felt that it was more important to promote education among Kashmiri women than her personal life. She founded Lowood Garden School, one of the few English Medium schools in Kashmir at that time. She focused on children from low-income groups, mostly the *Hanji* (boatmen) community, who were educated free of cost. For promoting girls' education, she would go house to house, motivating parents to send their daughters to her school. For this, she was widely known as Barkat Begum—one who brings forth good fortune and well being.

Many foreigners would take up temporary teaching assignments—even performing Shakespeare's plays—at Lowood Garden School. One of the many people who volunteered to teach in Lowood Garden School was Carol Jane Thatcher, a journalist, author and media personality, and most significantly, the daughter of the erstwhile Prime Minister of UK, Margaret Thatcher. She spent two successive summers in the late seventies in Srinagar. One of Barkat's grandsons, Sarmad Hafeez, Administrative Secretary, Tourism Department, remembers that

Barkat would distribute her pension among local boys. "Even in her old age, she refused to buy a car,) Hafeez says. "She said this kept her on par with her neighbours. Such was her concept of justice" (Handoo, Ref 5).

Agha Ashraf, grew up in an upper-class feudal household with a rich legacy of excellence, where education was a top priority. His mother Begum Zaffar Ali (described above), herself an educationist and a legislator was the first woman in Kashmir to pass the matriculation exam. Ashraf's elder brothers, Agha Nasir Ali and Agha Shaukat Ali, were both civil servants serving in India and Pakistan respectively. His maternal grandfather was the first matriculate of Kashmir and held a ministerial berth in the Maharaja's cabinet. Agha Ashraf's son is a celebrated Kashmiri American Poet, Agha Shahid Ali, who translated Faiz Ahmad Faiz's poetry in English. Unfortunately, he died in 2001. His other son Iqbal and daughters Hena and Sameetah are all settled in the US.

The famed educationist was instrumental in turning around the situation for Muslims in Kashmir after 1947. Agha became an inspector of schools at twenty-eight, whereas the median age for the post used to be fifty years. He recalls that at that time the entire education sector was dominated by Pandits. A number of schools were opened during those times, not only in Kashmir but in other parts of the state as well. In 1952, he went to Leh in a military plane sitting on a box to open the first primary school for girls in that region. He was then sent as an officiating principal of Teachers Training College, and that turned out to be the best phase of his life. Agha felt the dire need for good teachers and he took upon himself to do the job. He was successful in turning out the best teachers.

In 1960, Agha got a Fulbright Fellowship and went to

America for his PhD at Ball State University, Indiana. After his return to Kashmir, the University of Kashmir created a postgraduate department of education and he was the first Kashmiri to be selected as professor. In SP College, there were 1100 Pandit boys and just 111 Muslims and he felt deeply concerned about this gross difference. This prompted him to start the first Muslim block and he became its president. Similarly, during his tenure as principal of the Teachers Training College from 1955-60, there were 40 Pandit girls and just four Muslim girls but when he returned from the US in 1964, he found Muslim girls everywhere.

As Chairman of the Board of School Education, Agha Ashraf introduced compulsory mathematics and science in schools for all girls instead of traditional subjects like Home Science. He was a member of Baghwan Sahai Committee from 1971-75, and from 1973-75, he became Director of Training and Curricula. He always advocated teaching in Kashmiri and repeatedly called for the introduction of Kashmiri language at elementary level in all schools. He opined that those children, who are unfamiliar with their mother tongue, would find it difficult to learn other languages effectively.

Agha Ashraf is a good orator and an independent thinker, and has been lecturing in universities, colleges and schools after his retirement. On the eve of Teachers Day in 2006, he was awarded the *Nigeena–e–Watan* for his "unmatched contribution in the field of education." In 2011, he released his autobiography *Kuchh to Likhye ki log Kehte Hain* in Urdu, which has become an inspirational book (Mirani, Ref 20).

Today, after nearly eighty years, all the efforts made by the above-mentioned inspirational educationists have made a huge impact on the literacy level in the state. As per the

Census 2011, Jammu and Kashmir has a population of 12.5 million. The literacy level in Jammu and Kashmir climbed up from 11.3% in 1961 to 67.1 % in 2011, but it still lags far behind the national average of 74.4%. Further analysis of the data shows that male literacy rate is higher than female literacy rate in all the years. Male literacy rate increased from 16.9% in 1961 to 76.7% whereas the female literacy rate increased from 4.2% in 1961 to 56.4% in 2011. In the delineation of the figures above, it can be argued that though there is considerable progress in the female literacy rate, gender disparity in literacy and sex ratio (889 girls per 1000 boys) still exists with district wise variations.

Social Reforms

Historically, Kashmiri women were grossly suppressed during the Afghan and Sikh rule. Bazaz observes that enslavement of women was sanctioned and glorified in religious scriptures and being clean and well-dressed was looked at disdainfully. Education, cultural pursuits and fine arts were considered unnecessary. Amongst the Pandits, child marriage was the norm and widow remarriage was disallowed. Being a Rajput community, *Sati* was practiced by the Dogras and so was female infanticide.

By the decree of the Mughal emperors and the legislation enacted by the British Governor General, William Benting, *Sati* had been abolished in most parts of the country in 1835, but the Dogra Rajputs continued to observe this inhuman practice as Indian law was not applicable to the native states. As a measure of precaution, Maharaja Pratap Singh adopted an Act in 1916 to suppress *Sati* in the State but the roots of orthodoxy were so entrenched that it could not be abolished completely. Similarly, no concrete steps were taken by the rulers to control trafficking of women and prostitution. It is only the appointment of a British Resident Officer in the state that led to several changes in the condition of women in Kashmir. Maharaja Hari Singh promptly enacted the Sharda Act in 1929 (like in the rest of India) or the Child Marriage Restraint Act (named in honour of the social reformer Harbilas Sharda).

The Arya Samaj established in 1875 by Dayanand Saraswati, although stressing on reviving Vedic religion, was firmly rooted in the idea of changing the situation of women in various ways—improving literacy, preventing trafficking, child marriage and dowry; promoting widow remarriage and banning discrimination based on caste. In 1892, the Samaj set up four associations in Srinagar after remaining confined to Jammu for a long time. The Punjabi Hindus were instrumental in introducing it in the valley during their appointment in the state service. Kashmiri Hindus also joined this movement later to bring in social reforms purported by the Samaj in their own community (Kaur R).

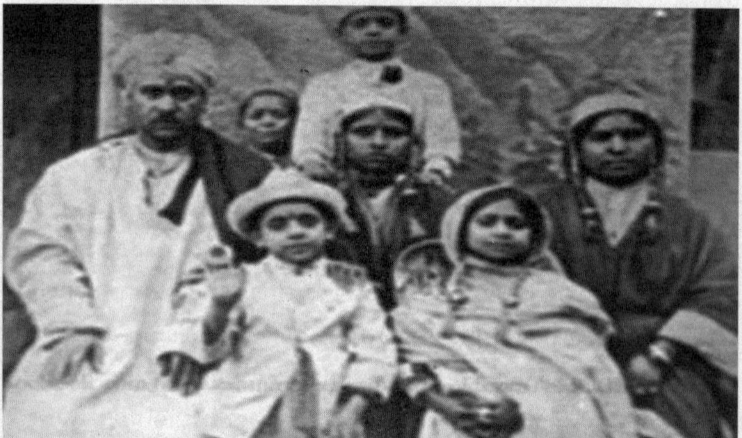

A Kashmiri Pandit child bride and groom

Transformation of Pandit Women—From Pheran to Saris

One of the strong proponents of the Arya Samaj was Tara Chand Bulbul, popularly known as Kashyap Bandhu, who revolutionised the mindset of Kashmiri Pandit community. He was born in 1899 in Gairu (Noorpur village, Tral, district Pulwama). After completing his schooling, he got a job in the revenue department. He went to Lahore where he got influenced by the ideology of Arya Samaj and returned to Kashmir to bring social reforms there. Bandhu joined the freedom movement spearheaded by Bhagat Singh and was arrested in the Sanders case but was released later. Some of his remarkable reforms included introduction of the sari and salwar kameez amongst Pandit women. As *Pheran* and *taranga* (traditional attire of Kashmiri Pandit women) with a *pooch* (covering on the head) was perceived to give rise to lethargy, and shackled women, Bandhu gradually steered the process of transformation. Initially, the idea received resistance, but when his volunteers engaged in door-to-door dialogue with every family, the women were convinced to adopt the new dress code. Eventually, this wave spread like wildfire and the *pheran* was soon replaced by sari and salwar kameez and women felt free and liberated without veils on their heads (Kaul,Ref 15).

At another level, Bandhu advocated for rights of Kashmiri labourers in Punjab. As a young boy in Lahore, he saw the miserable plight of the labourers who would migrate to various cities of Punjab in winter. The lived in shabby and squalid conditions, had unregulated working hours and were exploited by their employers. Wages were retained by their employers every time the labourers returned home after winter, forcing them to return to the same exploiter every year. Acting on the advice of Allama Iqbal (poet, philosopher and politician, who is

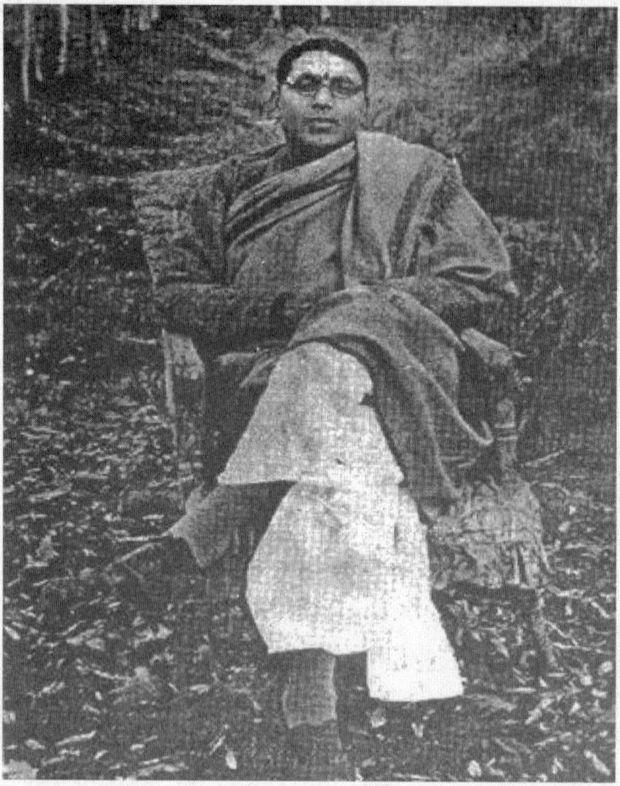

Kashyap Bandhu

widely regarded as having inspired the formation of Pakistan), whom he visited frequently, Bandhu became the first secretary of Kashmiri Mazdoor Board, Lahore, sometime around 1927 and worked for their rights.

Bandhu founded *Martand*, an Urdu publication and also edited *Desh* newspaper. He also headed the department of Rural Reconstruction during the prime ministership of Sheikh Mohammad Abdullah. He is also known to have helped the displaced Kashmiri Pandit villagers (victims of Pakistani tribal raiders in October 1947). Mota in his blog *Chinar Shade* has referred to him as Raja Ram Mohan Roy of Kashmir.

Bandhu also strongly opposed wasteful expenditure and unlimited number of guests during marriages. He and his colleagues used to sit on *dharnas* (protests) wherever such feasts were organised. He influenced people to limit the number of *baratis* (relatives and friends from the groom's side) and advocated for restriction on huge dowries. He promoted mass *Yajnopavita* (sacred thread) ceremony, one of the traditional rites of passage of Hindus. So strong was the reform movement that many marriages took place with just five *baratis* (Kaul).

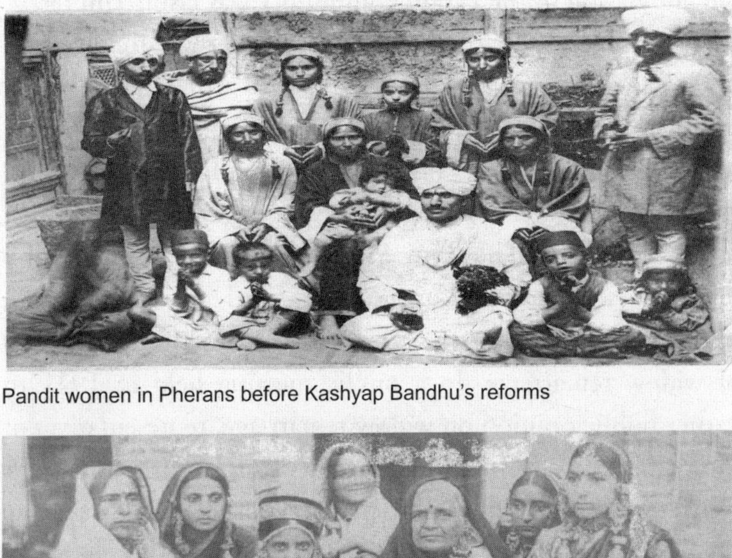

Pandit women in Pherans before Kashyap Bandhu's reforms

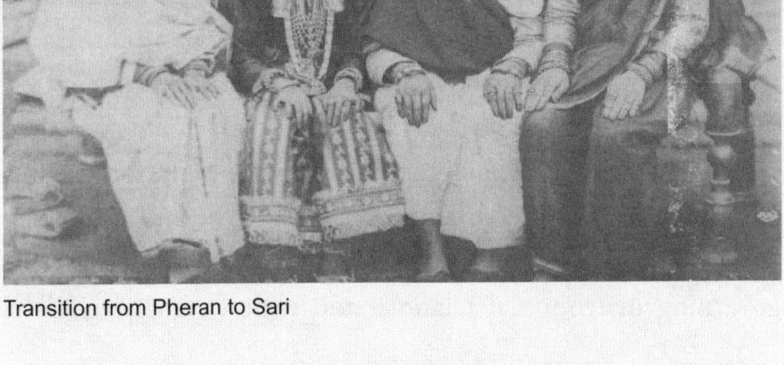

Transition from Pheran to Sari

Widow Remarriage

As per the 1921 census, Bazaz reports that widows formed 22% of the female population of the Pandit community and the proportion of males to females was 1000 to 821. Girls were married off when they were toddlers and if they lost their husbands early in childhood, they were doomed for life because widow remarriage was not permitted. They led joyless lives and were sexually exploited by their male relatives. With the declining sex ratio and nearly a quarter of the women widowed, the population of the Pandit community was fast declining.

In India, The Sati Prevention Act in 1829 followed by the Widow Remarriage Act in 1856 was a huge leap for the status of women. However, public opinion towards widow remarriage in Kashmir was hostile even till the early 1920s. If a widow did get remarried, her marriage was not deemed to be legitimate. The Arya Samaj as well as the Fraternity (another social uplift organisation) led by Chanderjoo, SK Toshkhani and Raghunath Mattoo were strong advocates of widow remarriage. In a public meeting held in 1931 to garner public opinion on widow remarriage, representatives of the community from various departments and organisations were invited and a heated discussion took place between the liberals who were part of Fraternity and the orthodox elements. The orthodox elements identified themselves with 'Sanatan Dharma' (Traditional Hinduism) and they upheld that widow remarriage was against the basic tenets of Hinduism.

The fight continued and the orthodox elements led by a prominent lawyer, Amar Nath Kak, got a resolution passed, denouncing the memorandum passed by the Maharaja. They demanded that no changes be made to the Hindu code governing matrimonial relations and widow remarriage. The

Fraternity educated the public about the deplorable condition of widows—their large number, poor social and economic status, incidence of abortion, sexual exploitation, prostitution and its negative impact on the already declining population of the community. Finally, in 1933, legislation against widow remarriage was passed in the state. Kashyap Bandhu also made a great contribution to this cause. Many of his young followers married widows from the Kashmiri Pandit community. Besides opening tailoring centres for the widows, his volunteers visited each and every house to collect rice for economically and socially backward widows. They called it *Mochchi Phol* (a fistful) of rice as a token contribution.

Trafficking of Women

Sharma & Rana, (Ref 31) have described at length the state of prostitution in Kashmir. According to them, the practice was in vogue in ancient Kashmir and seems to have been prevalent throughout the medieval period as well. The beautiful girls of Kashmir remained objects of attraction and possession during the Mughal Period (1586-1752 CE), and the Pathan regime (1752-1819 CE). It was the lure of Kashmiri women that brought into existence regular trafficking, particularly from 1586 onwards. With the arrival of the Dogras, the trade continued to flourish openly, and early Dogra rulers patronised this disreputable trade and acquired a sizeable amount of revenue from it. Although the government derived a lot of income from the prostitutes, nothing was spent for their betterment. They remained untreated during sickness as there was no Lock hospital in Kashmir and, as a result, a syphilitic disease had spread terribly throughout the state. It was only in 1912 that both Europeans and Indians voiced their disgust at this practice, which was being followed brazenly in public and legalised through a system of taxation. As per Parimoo, it was Subhan Hajam, a barber from Maisuma, Srinagar, who raised a cry against the practice and succeeded in mobilising public opinion for eradication of prostitution in Kashmir. Dr Fida Hussain further adds that it was Maulvi Mohammad Abdullah Vakil (freedom fighter for Kashmir's independence from Maharaja's rule and prominent lawyer born in the late nineteenth century) who raised the issue in the Praja Sabha in 1934 and proposed exacting of a law for the closure of prostitution houses in the state. The Maharaja finally issued orders banning sale and purchase of women in the state and closure of red-light areas in Srinagar and Jammu.

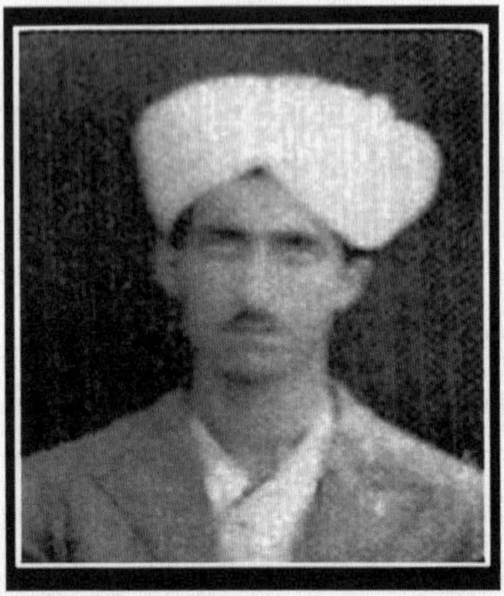

Subhan Hajam

In 1944, under the Naya Kashmir framework (headed by Sheikh Mohammad Abdullah and prepared by BPL Bedi and other communist members) a democratic Constitution committed to the welfare of common people of Kashmir became operational. The idea of equality of opportunity for women was created and incorporated into the Jammu and Kashmir Constitution in 1956 under Section 22. This step provided a portal for women to enter the mainstream of all areas of social, economic and political life of the state.

Securing the Rights of Manual Scavengers

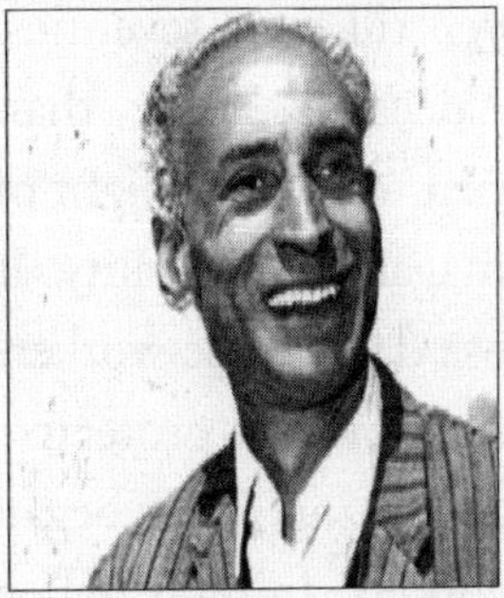

Hriday Nath Wanchoo

If Bindeshwar Pathak fought against manual scavenging in Bihar in the sixties and seventies, Hriday Nath Wanchoo did so for sanitation workers (*safai karamcharis*) in Srinagar, Kashmir. Wanchoo was born in a family of academicians and technocrats on 24th May, 1925 at Maliyar, Habba Kadal. His father Keshav Nath Wanchoo was a government employee in the judicial department and mother Leelavati was a homemaker. He received his primary education from Ganesh Ghat School and later passed his matriculation from SP School, Fateh Kadal. Wanchoo joined SP College and obtained his degree from Lahore University. During his college career, he was actively involved in student politics and also associated with various organisations fighting for social equality, rights of the downtrodden, right to health and sanitation. He also actively participated in the Quit Kashmir Movement, which was headed at the time by J&K National Conference founder Sheikh Mohammad Abdullah. Because of his active involvement he got arrested and was jailed for around a year. He was put in detention at various jails of Jammu and Kashmir.

After his release, Wanchoo joined the Red Cross Society. He started many projects and schemes for the welfare of the people of J&K. He was supported by various renowned doctors of that time like Dr Thusoo, Dr Shangloo and Dr Ali Jan.

Although key legislations were enacted in 1933 prohibiting employment of people as manual scavengers (who collect, carry and dispose human waste from dry latrines), banning construction of dry latrines and providing rehabilitation, this practice was in operation in Srinagar even till early seventies. Wanchoo, who was born nearly two decades earlier than Pathak, was deeply disturbed and saddened to see the plight of the sanitation workers employed in Srinagar Municipality. It was a period of awakening for him. Those days, these workers had to carry all human waste on their heads with no protective measures to safeguard their health and well-being. Thus began the movement for the rights of these workers. Initially, when the State government did not take them seriously, Wanchoo organised a protest wherein workers collected all the human waste of the city and put it in front of the secretariat. After a long struggle they won. Their major achievements included regular salary, insurance cover on duty, employment of a family member in case of eventuality, proper dress code, proper tools and health benefits. Committed to providing dignity to these invisible workers, Wanchoo started the concept of an emergency fund for them as well as other labour classes. Through his efforts, a school was started at Batamaloo for the workers' children wherein they were provided free books and uniforms, and teachers offered free services. The pass-outs from this school are doing quite well in various sectors within and outside the state.

Later, he founded the Srinagar Municipal Employees Union and organised the entire municipality in Srinagar and Jammu taking it to district level. He was instrumental in bringing the concept of co-operatives in Kashmir and established co-operative stores.

He joined the Communist Party of India after his retirement from Srinagar Municipality and became its general secretary in Kashmir. His rich experience and human rights approach made him a pioneer of workers' movement and trade unions in the state, and he was the founder of the Human Rights movement in the state. He also worked a lot for the uplift of labourers working in mining and other industries with high occupational hazards.

He was appointed Secretary General of All India Trade Union Congress (body of workers), General Secretary for Kashmir Council for All India Peace and Solidarity, Director Indo-USSR Friendship Society, Director Indo-German Democratic Society, Trade Unions co-coordinator South Asia for Moscow, Czechoslovakia, France, Poland, Egypt, Iran and many other countries.

That he was a great advocate of communal harmony was noticed when he extended help to people from various communities during the separatist movement in 1989-90. Wanchoo formed the Hindu Welfare Forum, wherein he attempted to bridge the gap between the two communities. Similarly, he raised his voice against all those who indulged in killing, disappearance, torture and extortion. It was due to his efforts that international organisations like Amnesty International, Asia Watch and many others took note of human rights violations in Kashmir post 1990.

However, on 5th December 1992, at 10:15 am,Wanchoo was killed in cold blood at Balgarden, Karan Nagar, Srinagar by separatists and thus ended the legacy of the greatest humanitarian of all times (Wanchoo, Ref 36).

Section 2

Deathly Dark Nights

The Summer of 1990 That Never Was

I WAS married in 1987 in Srinagar and migrated to the hot plains of India as my husband was a second-generation migrant; his father had left Srinagar in search of employment in Delhi in the mid-fifties. I was pregnant with my first child in August 1989 and had dreams of having my delivery in Srinagar as the due date was in mid-May 1990 when it is scorching in the plains of India. But what emerged after the killing of Tikalal Taploo and others post September 1989 seemed like a never-ending nightmare. Assuming the situation to be short-term and not really directed towards Pandits, we continued to make plans for the summer of 1990. However, our plans soon fell through when my family in Kashmir also received warnings to leave the valley.

On January 4, 1990, a local Urdu newspaper *Aftab* published a press release issued by *Hizb-ul-Mujahideen*, asking all Pandits to leave the valley immediately. Another local paper, *Al Safa*, repeated this expulsion order. The miniscule community had been facing death threats earlier, but on January 19, 1990, the umbilical cord with *Maej Kashir* (mother Kashmir) was finally severed when more than three lakh Kashmiri Pandits left the valley after being openly threatened through inflammatory speeches broadcasted from the public address systems of the mosques. The night of 19th January 1990 has been permanently embedded in the psyche of every Kashmiri Pandit who had to flee from his motherland to never return.

According to a report by the Jammu and Kashmir government, as many as 219 people from the Pandit community were killed in the region between 1989 and 2004. The Kashmir Pandit Sangharsh Samiti (KPSS) after carrying out a survey in 2008 and 2009 said that 399 Kashmiri Pandits were killed by insurgents from 1990 to 2011, with 75% of them killed during the first year of the Kashmiri insurgency. The Samiti estimates that about 650 Pandits have been killed in the valley over the past 20 years, and 357 Pandits were killed in 1990 alone.

Several authors have penned accounts and personal experiences of the exodus over the years. What remains common in these descriptions is the terror that gripped the night of 19th January. Here's an excerpt of Col Tej Kumar Tikoo's book (2013), *Kashmir: Its Aborigines and Their Exodus*, describing the fateful night:

> As the night fell, the microscopic community became panic-stricken when the Valley began reverberating with the war-cries of fundamentalists, who had stage-managed

> the whole event with great care; choosing its timing and the slogans to be used. A host of highly provocative, communal and threatening slogans, interspersed with martial songs, incited the Muslims to come out on the streets and break the chains of 'slavery'. These exhortations urged the faithful to give a final push to the *Kafirs* in order to ring in the true Islamic order. These slogans were mixed with precise and unambiguous threats to Pandits. They were presented with three choices—*Ralive, Tsaliv ya Galive* (convert to Islam, leave the place or perish). Tens of thousands of Kashmiri Muslims poured into the streets of the Valley shouting 'death to India' and 'death to *Kafirs*'.... For the Kashmiri Pandits, the Seventh Exodus[4] was staring them in the face.

The above excerpt presents the sordid reality of the Pandit story. However, the discourse that has been commonly circulated amongst the local Kashmiris is that the exodus was stage managed by the then governor, Jagmohan, who encouraged the Pandits to flee the valley, leaving only Muslims so that they could be exterminated by the army. Others claim that it was done only by misled youth in a few masjids. Every Kashmiri Pandit who has lived through that experience will deny such claims. The fact that 3,50,000 Pandits left en-mass indicates the fear and terror that was unleashed in the valley at that time.

The fundamentalist wave did not spare the Muslims also. Those who were suspected to have allegiance to India were targeted—the National Conference ministers, politicians

4 Historically, Kashmiri Pandits have been forced to leave the valley six times earlier due to terror and forced conversion from Muslim rulers from 14th to 18th century. In 1990, it was the seventh exodus.

and *mukhbirs* (informers). However, there is no official data available regarding the number of Muslims that migrated outside the valley.

The fundamentalists were successful in dividing the Pandit and Muslim communities who shared the same language, literature, music and food habits creating a rich symbiotic culture. Most importantly, they destroyed the mutual trust that the two communities had shared since centuries.

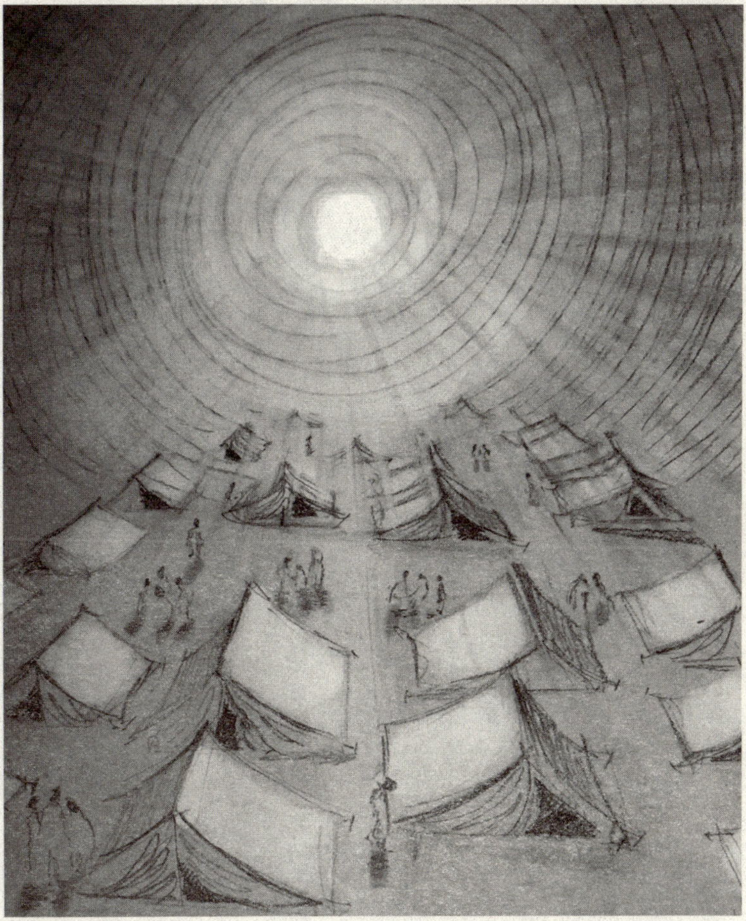

A Migrant Camp

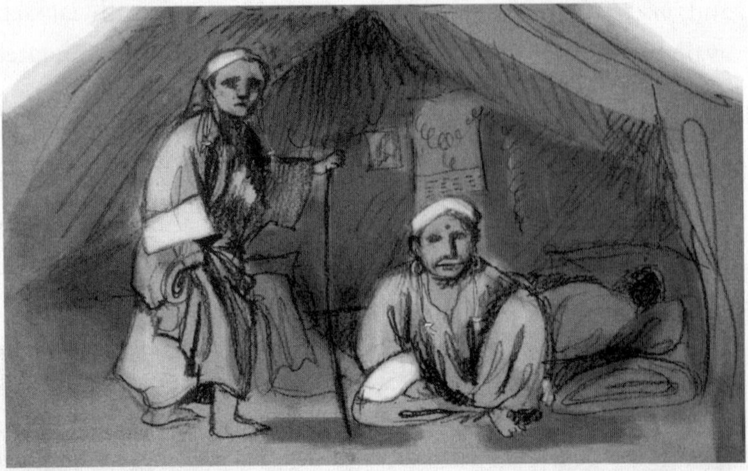

Life at a refugee camp

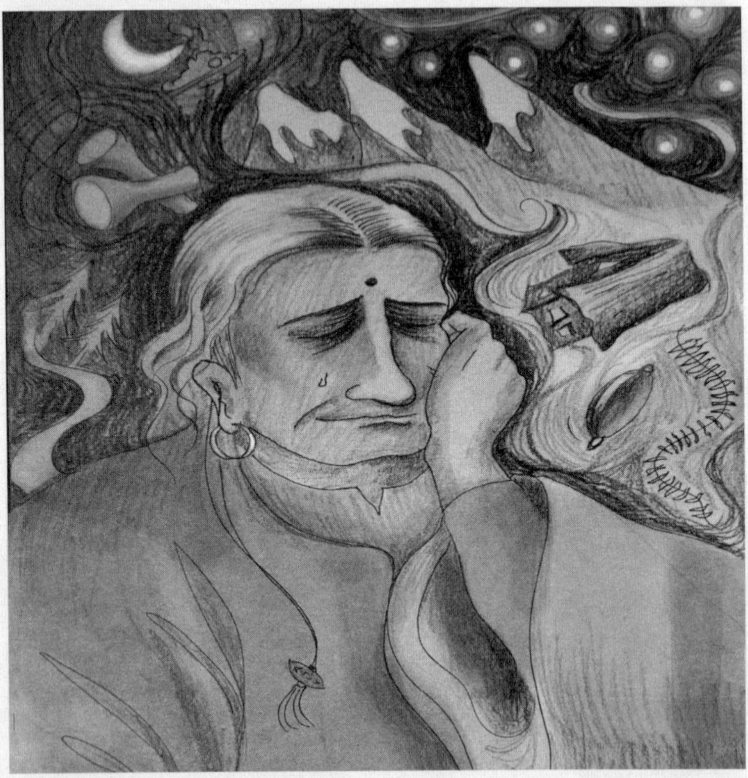

Traumatised, uprooted and homeless

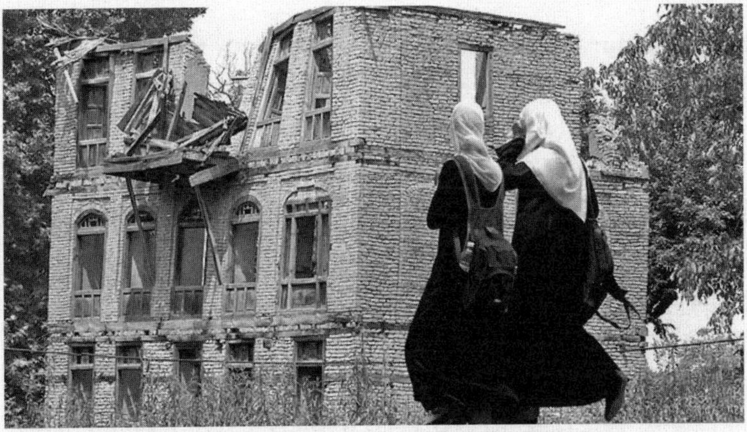

A dilapidated Kashmiri Pandit house (sourced from the internet)

Growth of Rights-based Organisations for Pandits

Panun Kashmir is an organisation of displaced/refugee Kashmiri Pandits (Hindus) founded in December 1990 in Jammu. They demand a separate state or union territory as a means to protect themselves from attacks by separatist militants, while at the same time preserving Kashmiri Hindu culture. The organisation wishes for displaced Hindus to be termed as refugees rather than migrants, which they allege is a term used by the state administration for their community. The organisation claims that its goal is broad enough to not only encompass the cause of Kashmir's Hindus, but also India's survival and territorial integrity. *Panun Kashmir* recognises Kashmir's Muslim majority as formerly Hindu who were forced to convert to Islam. This resulted in the Hindu population becoming a minority because they were either killed or forced out of Kashmir. It wants Kashmir's existing Hindu population to be considered as native inhabitants of Kashmir. The organisation advocates that cities such as Anantnag, Sopore, Baramulla and Avantipur be included in the Kashmiri Hindu homeland. It seeks a homeland for Kashmiri Pandits who are ready to live peacefully with their Muslim neighbours. However, after 28 years, none of their demands have been fulfilled. (Wikipedia, n.d.)

Roots In Kashmir is another initiative launched by Kashmiri Pandit Youth to reclaim their roots. Even though they have been hounded out of their homes and hearths in Kashmir, their roots are very much anchored in the Vitasta (ancient name of River Jhelum) Valley. This is an initiative to protest and raise the general awareness of the public to a level where the "fight for our roots" is felt, heard and acted upon (*Roots In Kashmir, n.d.*).

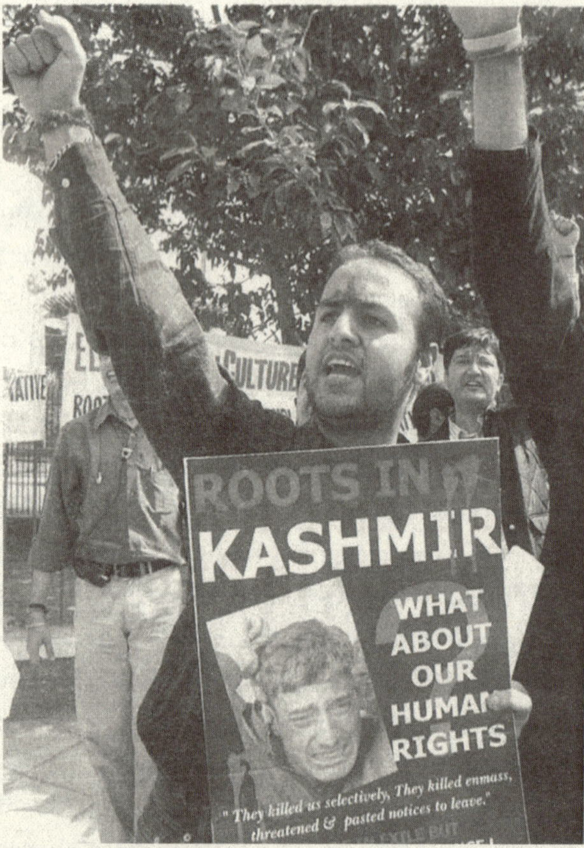

(Sourced from the internet)

Impact of the Azadi Movement and Militancy

Fall of Educational Institutions and Public infrastructure: According to Tikoo (Ref 35), around 725 educational institutions and 303 bridges and culverts were destroyed in Kashmir between 1989 and 1996. Schools and colleges were targeted; carefully built-up libraries and laboratories went up in flames. The auditorium of Women's College, which had been witness to the students' achievements through the ages, was torched.

During the years of turmoil from 1989 to 2016, educational establishments have faced tough trials and the test of time. The recent unrest in Kashmir, which broke out after the killing of Hizbul Commander, Burhan Wani, triggered protests across the valley. In 2016, about 27 government schools were burned down. One news item comments, "*The separatists and the fundamentalists in the Kashmir Valley are determined to turn back the clock and take the Valley once again to the medieval era where the Maulvis and Qazis ruled the roost and their writ ran unchallenged.*" (*Indo-Asian News Service,* 2016).

Introduction of Hijab and Control on Women's Freedom

Those who have seen the era of seventies and early eighties can testify to the gross regressive change in the dress code and mobility of women. Most people, especially middle aged or older women say that during their time it was common to see Muslim girls covering their heads with a *dupatta* (a long scarf) in colleges and offices but it was rare to find women dressed up in *burqas*. Sudden radicalisation of the dress code took place in the nineties and soon almost everybody was wearing the *hijab* and *abaya.*

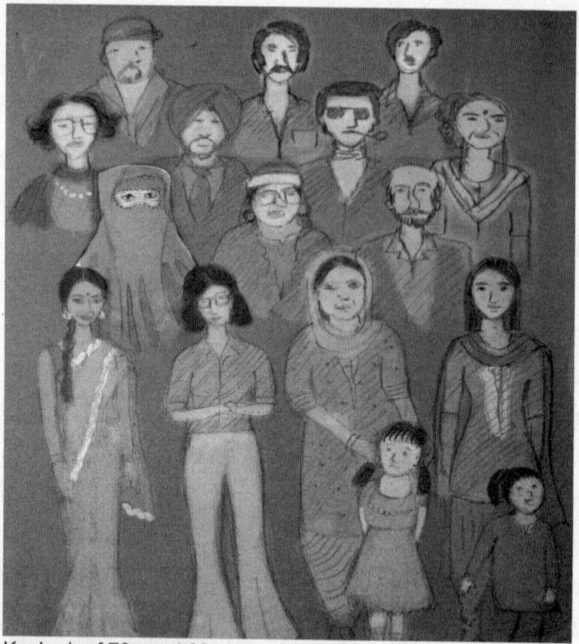

Kashmir of 70s and 80s

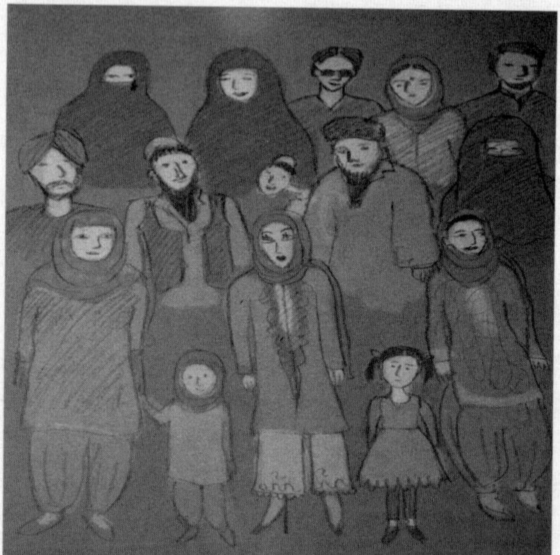

The changing face of Kashmir post 1990s

Closure of Cinema Houses

As I pass by the dilapidated structure that was once Palladium Cinema in Lal Chowk, Srinagar, I excitedly tell the young cab driver about the fun we had watching our favourite movies here. He turns around and says wistfully, "*Madam, ase chuna su zamana vuchmuth*" (madam we have not seen that era). I suddenly realise that I am talking to a 25-year old boy who has never watched a movie in a theatre in Srinagar. An article that appeared in *The Daily Brief* by Scroll.in on December 14th 2017, gives a vivid description of the fate of cinema in the state:

> The eruption of militancy in the 1990s brought the curtains down on 19 cinema halls in Kashmir, including 9 in Srinagar. Today, most of the theatres are camps for security forces, while others have been turned into hotels, shopping complexes and even a hospital. But they live on in the memories of the people who still remember the joy of going to the movies. Everything changed as the valley plunged into chaos in the summer of 1989. As Islamist militants took over the streets within a matter of months, the campaign against what they deemed un-Islamic intensified. Among the first diktats was a ban on liquor vends and cinema halls, issued by Allah Tigers, a radical outfit. Amidst threats and intimidation, the vendors and cinemas shut down one after another. As the government started pushing in troops to suppress the militancy, bunkers made an appearance in the abandoned cinema halls. By 1994, these venues of entertainment had become some of the most dreaded places in the Valley—home to camps formally called interrogation centres but more commonly known as torture chambers.

The article further observes that in 1999, three cinema halls—Regal, Neelam and Broadway—were reopened. That same year in September, militants attacked Regal with grenades, killing one moviegoer and injuring twelve. In September 2005, Neelam—the only operational movie theatre in Srinagar by then—was the stage for an encounter between the police and suicide attackers in which one militant was killed. Around seventy people were in the theatre at the time watching the Aamir Khan-starrer *Mangal Pandey*. Going to the movies became dangerous, and the taboo associated with it was very strong.

However, after the nineties, people switched over to television and computer screens to watch movies. Sales of televisions, VCRs and video cassettes picked up. Later, video CDs and DVDs became popular. The pirated movie trade flourished until the advent of the internet when people started downloading movies. Video cassette dealers were also threatened in the 1990s and bans were issued by militant organisations. Some even witnessed grenade attacks, but they continued with their business. Despite the risks, customers still come to these shops. During the unrest of 2016, pirated copies of DVDs were in demand since people had nothing to do, and the internet was banned. With political turmoil and unrest following years of militancy, many Kashmiris no longer mourn the movie halls. The small screen and internet have been their saviour.

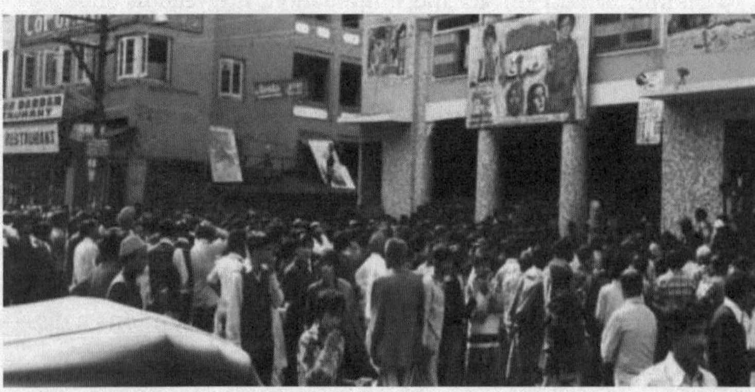

Then: Palladium Cinema during its heyday

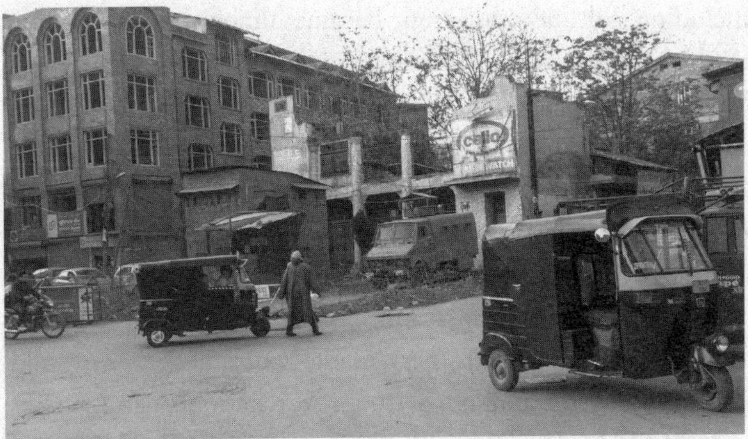

Now: Palladium cinema house in ruins. It houses a bunker for security forces

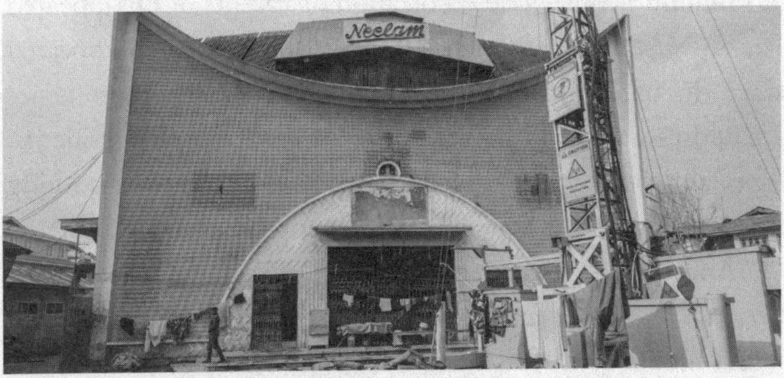

Neelam cinema shut and abandoned

Birth of a Culturally Impoverished Generation

Tagore Hall, the nerve-centre of cultural activities in Kashmir, was recently renovated after being destroyed by a bomb blast in 1990. In the early days of the resistance movement, militants bombed Tagore Hall to send the message that the population should not participate in cultural activities, as they were considered 'un-Islamic'.

As per a report published in *Indian Press Service* (IPS), Srinagar, on December 4, 2012, the heavy impact of conflict and insecurity crushed normal life. So, education of all types, including cultural education, became almost impossible due to the presence of the Indian army and frequent encounters between army personnel and militants. Abdul Gani Madhosh, a former professor at Kashmir University reports that the Academy of Art, Culture and Languages, which used to organise cultural programmes in the Kashmir Valley prior to 1989 was forced to cease its operations.

"The conflict simply killed cultural life in Kashmir," Farhat Lone, a special officer in the Cultural Academy told IPS. Tens of thousands of troops are stationed at intervals across Indian-administered Kashmir to oversee a population of 7.5 million people. The Association of Parents of Disappeared Persons (APDP) says that 10,000 people have disappeared since the inception of militancy in 1989. Unless these issues are addressed, it will be very difficult for Kashmir's residents, especially the younger generation which has known nothing but war, to find the time for cultural appreciation.

Another article that appeared on Dec 5, 2012 (*Indian Press Service*), reports about the survey conducted by the New Delhi based Indian Trust for Art and Cultural Heritage (INTACH). Based on extensive interviews with a sample population of 1,600 people, combined with a broad field research, this survey found a significant "cultural disconnect" in 98% of the youth polled. "We are most concerned about the fact that the majority of the respondents were unaware about the rich cultural heritage of Kashmir," Saleem Beig, who headed INTACH in Jammu and Kashmir at that time told *IPS*. The study indicates that the youth are ignorant about the world-renowned religious and architectural sites in the region. According to the survey, "a majority of the respondents could not even describe what cultural heritage was and felt that they should be educated about it by the media and local government." The survey also found that 91% of inhabitants view cultural heritage as the practice of traditional crafts like carpet weaving, shawl making, papier mâché, embroidery and woodcarving. Experts like late Dabla (Ref 7) blamed this worrying trend on the ravages of conflict, which has its roots in the 1947 partition of India.

Tourism

As per Directorate of Statistics, Goverenment of Jammu and Kashmir's 2015 report, the number of tourists visiting the state in 1980 and 1985 was nearly 6 lakhs and 5.3 lakhs respectively, which slid lower in the nineties. It reduced to 8,500 in 1995 then went up to 16,500 in 1997. However, due to better conditions after 2004, tourist inflow touched an all-time high of 13.14 lakhs in 2011. In 2016 and 2017, tourism faced a huge setback again. Thus, we see that due to insurgency and unstable conditions, tourism has failed to be a dependable source of revenue for the people of the state.

Widows and Orphans on the Rise

Widows and orphans represent a group that has suffered a lot in present-day Kashmir; it has emerged mainly because of the armed conflict between Kashmiri militants and Indian security forces from 1989 onwards. The study conducted by Kashmir University, "A Sociological Study of Widows & Orphans in Kashmir, 2016", spearheaded by late Prof Bashir Ahmad Dabla, head of the Department of Sociology, reveals that there are 32,400 widows and 97,000 to 1 lakh orphans in the valley. It says the sudden death of male members has shattered thousands of families leaving behind impoverished and emotionally traumatised widows and orphans. This unfortunate loss of society is due to ex-local militants and the common-civilian population who were killed either by security forces or died in armed encounters between militants and forces. The study revealed that the situation of widows and orphans is pathetic and miserable. Absence of accommodation, poor economic conditions, educational backwardness, ill-health, mass depression, deviance and delinquency amongst children, social disorganisation and disorder, insecurity, and total dependence on others were some of the major problems faced by this group. This study further asserts "Neither State nor NGOs have been able to help them in an organised and systematic manner. The tragic aspect of the situation is that the State has not adopted any specific social policy and programme in this regard. Their problems accumulate and intensify day-by-day. Individuals, society, community and the State must share responsibilities in terms of coordination, organisation and effective implementation of relevant programs".

Debilitating Mental Health

Years of armed conflict and the heavily militarised environment has taken an emotional toll on the State's population. The 2015 Kashmir Mental Health Survey conducted by the international humanitarian organisation, *Doctors without Borders*, found that 45% of adults in the Kashmir valley display major symptoms of mental distress, with about one in five adults, or 19% of the adult population, displaying major symptoms of post-traumatic stress disorder (PTSD). The survey put the prevalence of depression in adults at 41%. In contrast, the National Mental Health Survey of India 2015-16 puts the prevalence of depression at the all-India level in single digits. The National Crime Bureau Records reveal that States that had a significant percentage increase in suicides in 2015 over 2014 were Uttarakhand (129.5%), Meghalaya (73.7%), Lakshadweep (66.7%), Nagaland (61.5%) and Jammu & Kashmir (44.2%). The article *Menace of Social Evils* in *Kashmir Reader* mentions that the rising graph blemishes the social and cultural integrity of the State (Sugra, Ref 34). Gender delineation reveals that 62 percent of the suicides in the valley involved women while men comprised 38 percent. The reason is very obvious. Women have been the silent sufferers of the ongoing turmoil in Kashmir (Dabla).

Sugra further reports that other problems that plague Kashmiri society today are dowry and extravagance in marriages that particularly impact girls from poorer classes. Also, issues like molestation, drug addiction and moral degradation need to be addressed.

Allocation of Funds and Corruption in J&K

According to *The Hindu,* Jammu and Kashmir has received 10% of all Central grants given to States over the 2000-2016 period, despite having only one percent of the country's population. In contrast, Uttar Pradesh makes up about 13% of the country's population but received only 8.2% of Central grants during 2000-2016. That means J&K, with a population of 12.55 million according to the 2011 Census, received Rs 91,300 per person over the last sixteen years, while Uttar Pradesh only received Rs 4,300 per person over the same period.The seeming imbalance in Jammu and Kashmir's finances—with Central grants accounting for 54% of the State's total revenue and 44% of its expenditure in FY16—assumes significance in light of the fact that the Comptroller and Auditor General of India in 2015 castigated the Jammu and Kashmir government for the pendency of a large number of inspection reports and observations highlighting "serious financial irregularities" in the state. Jammu and Kashmir is also among the worst hit states in India when it comes to corruption, says a survey conducted by Centre for Media studies (CMS) in its *India Corruption Study* 2017. Jammu and Kashmir is placed with Karnataka, Tamil Nadu, and Andhra Pradesh as the most corrupt states. Karnataka (77%), Andhra Pradesh (74%), Tamil Nadu (68%) Maharashtra (57%), Jammu and Kashmir (44%) and Punjab (42%) are some of the states where people experience corruption in public services.

A recent article in *Kashmir Reader* (2018), reports that in 2013, the government had said that by 2021, Jammu and Kashmir will be an energy surplus state, after giving the nod to nearly 6000 MW capacity of hydro power projects, the majority of which were to be constructed on the Chenab River in Jammu region. In 2018, work has begun on one power project while six are still undergoing paper work.

Regarding educational institutions, Kashmir has no dearth of post-graduate institutions. Prominent ones are: Sheri Kashmir Institute of Medical Services (SKIMS), Dental College, Veterinary College, Agricultural University, Regional Engineering College, Artificial Limb Centre, Institute of Hotel Management and Physical Training Institute.

The data given above indicates that the state has received ample resources, yet it is being claimed that the people of Kashmir are impoverished and lacking in resources. Looking at the educational infrastructure, health institutes, road and power projects of the state, questions can be raised about lack of accountability and the failure of public institutions in fulfilling their obligations to its citizens.

Unemployment amongst Youth

In his article, 'Menace of Social Evils' (*Kashmir Reader*, 2017), Sugra mentions that over three lakh educated youngsters have registered themselves at the employment exchange. The challenge of unemployment is not limited to Kashmir Valley alone. A recent article that appeared in *The Times of India* (April 3, 2018) titled 'India's Failing Education System' by Anustup Nayak mentions that less than 17% of India's graduates are employable as per the Annual Status of Education (ASER) report. There will soon be 100 million under-skilled and under-employed young people on our streets. Many will be desperate, leading them to harass, loot and molest, or harm themselves if not others. A student commits suicide every hour in India, unable to fulfill aspirations, cope with failure or find emotional support, according to *India Spend* reports.

These figures are worrying for our youth, especially Kashmiri youth who are facing conflicts and disturbances in their everyday life. The more we exclude them from the mainstream Indian state, the more they will get polarised and alienated. One of my Kashmiri (Muslim) friend's daughter studying in Delhi says, "My friends tell me that I am anti-India and I am a fundamentalist. I feel very disturbed and sad. My interaction with them is very little now." As more and more Kashmiri Muslim students spread themselves over the country and the world, their identity will always be haunted by the history of their original land of birth and the separatist ideology. On the other hand, Kashmiri Pandit youth are alienated from their land of ancestors, unaware of the legacy of their rich past. A past that has been marred by the agonising collective memories of their parents of the *Paradise Lost*.

SECTION 3

The Bravehearts and Rebuilders

WHEN DEATH was waiting at the corner and the sun was setting for most Pandits, a few bravehearts held on and faced the worst. Can anyone imagine their psyche when most of the minority community was gone and Islamic fundamentalism was at its peak? How did they survive? These heroes held on with a never-say-die attitude. In doing so, they gave hope to lakhs of Pandits languishing in refugee camps in Jammu and Delhi and kept the fire of Kashmiryat burning. They were the only link to the Pandits outside and gave the message that "all is not lost; we are saving our sinking ships". Many Pandits outside the valley viewed their wish to hold on with suspicion. Some thought they stuck around for their properties while others thought that they had been converted and were paying the extortionists (militants) to survive in the valley. These heroes are the only reason for some Pandits to visit their homeland, assuaging their fears with a message of hope for the reclamation of their home.

The short biographies given below are by no means exhaustive, but provide a glimpse of the darkest period in Kashmir. The first sub-section Bravehearts deals with the stories of courageous Pandit women who stood their ground and never left their homeland. The second sub-section Rebuilders describes the important contribution of educationists, peace builders, rehabilitators and healers, preservers of art, culture and literature, environmentalists and sports promoters for youth in the climate of conflict and fear.

The Bravehearts

Khemlata Wakhlu: The first woman politician who won with love, faith and dignity

Khemlata was born in 1936 in Srinagar to Pandit Niranjan Nath Dhar, an Income Tax Commissioner and his wife, Shrimati Tarawati. Khemlata feels privileged to be born in a family that was ahead of its time. She has five siblings: three brothers and two sisters. Her grandfather, Ramchandra Dhar, was the first graduate in J&K in the early 19th century. He was brought up and educated in Lucknow till the age of twenty-five, and was greatly influenced by Motilal Nehru during the freedom movement. Much against his wishes, he was compelled to return to Srinagar because of property disputes with his cousins. His decision to stay back in the valley turned out to be the biggest blessing for the family, as he completely changed their thinking with his radical ideology. He was a great visionary who emphasised that both girls and boys should be educated and given equal opportunities to develop themselves. He impacted not only his family (his five sons, three daughters and their children), but also his extended family comprising of his second and third cousins and their grandchildren. He was respected by one and all in Kashmir. Khemlata observes:

> It would not be an exaggeration to say that he impacted the Kashmiri Pandit community as a whole. We in Kashmir were *pathkun* (backward), behind the mountains and geographically inaccessible with no communication with the outside world. The seeds of modernism and a progressive outlook were sown by my grandfather.

Khemlata joined Vasanta Girls School (predominantly flocked by Pandit girls) like most girls at that time. Her grandfather was very particular that apart from academics, children irrespective of their gender should learn music and do physical exercise. The family house was a scene to behold—her cousins (brothers and sisters) sharing the same space, exercising, taking part in dramatics and learning to play the sitar together. Her younger aunt, Gauri Dhar Saraf was also the first woman to pass the matriculation exam. Although her elder aunt never went to school, she was well-versed in Persian. She adds that even her grandmother would recite couplets in Persian and converse in elementary Persian. As a child, Khemlata was a rebel of sorts—when asked to get a glass of water for her brother, she would protest. She was sensitive and felt disturbed about the inequalities in society, like sweepers having to carry human waste on their heads in Jammu or giving separate food to Muslims. When Dr Girija Dhar (a distant cousin) married a Muslim, there was a huge outcry in the family. Khemlata would debate and discuss the issue with members of her family and coax them to accept Dr Girija's decision.

Regardless of the progressive family climate, her parents were looking keenly for a 'suitable' and good boy for Khemlata, a difficult task even in that era. They spotted Omkarnath Wakhlu, a young lad, who was studying in the first year of the Bachelor of Engineering course at the Benares Hindu University (BHU). Khemlata had passed her Prabhakar exam (The equivalent of matriculation and graduation) before her marriage. She was preparing for her intermediate exam privately due to her father's transfer to Jammu. At that time, being a student and a teenager was not considered to be a deterrent for marriage. So, the teenage couple got married in 1952. Omkarnath later pursued his doctorate and became the principal of the then Regional Engineering College, now National Institute of Technology (NIT), Srinagar.

At the age of 15, Khemlata had no idea what marriage meant, but she was thrilled to wear nice clothes. However, she continued to practise the sitar. She had two sons and in 1960, Omkarnath, along with the family went to Birmingham, England. Undeterred by the responsibility of raising two children, Khemlata pursued a diploma in Home Science. In 1964 they returned to Srinagar. She loved writing about her experiences and soon started writing books and poetry. The Wakhlu family then went to Germany where she became a member of the Indo-German Society and YWCA. Her involvement, however, was limited as her children were young and needed her attention. On her return from Germany, she started taking interest in the political scene in Kashmir and India. Both she and her husband were radical thinkers and keen on bringing societal changes but were always in a dilemma—who would earn and how would they sustain their family? She was also aware that a woman politician would have trouble being accepted in a conservative society like Kashmir where women lived in fear and weren't free to exercise their choices. But she always had the inner calling "to do something".

Khemlata and Omkarnath met Sheikh Mohammad Abdullah (leader of the National Conference, Srinagar) in Delhi. He motivated them to do something for Kashmir and not waste their education in foreign countries. That was the turning point and beginning of her political journey.

Khemlata stood for her first election as an independent candidate in 1971. Though she lost the election it was a good experience for her and she learnt a lot. She joined the NC (National Conference) and gradually understood the workings of a political party. Gradually, she progressed from a Provincial Secretary to Provincial President and finally the Women's Wing President. Her close contact with the masses was an eye-opening experience for her. She faced religious fundamentalists and other opposition with aplomb and grace. She remarks that there have been many women rulers in the past like Queen Didda and Kota Rani, but she was the first Pandit minister in the modern era. She became the Minister of Tourism from 1983-87, but due to ideological differences with the NC, Khemlata left the party and joined the Congress in 2000.

She operated silently because she was constantly being threatened by separatist groups. Nonetheless, she showed supreme courage by entering into open dialogue with separatists and explained to them the futility of the idea of *azadi* due to the absence of a single leader of the people they claimed to represent. Dreams of *azadi* would have become a reality during the time of Sheikh Abdullah, who was an influential and towering personality, but who would listen to the separatists now? Even Pandits could have participated in the struggle for *azadi* but instead, the separatists killed the Pandits and drove the rest of this intellectual class away and transformed their so-called fight for self-determination into a bloody war for an Islamic state.

That she was a woman of grit and steel was revealed when Khemlata and her husband were kidnapped in 1991. During the period of their captivity (45days), they were constantly moved to different locations. They have written a book on their experiences and the accounts give a glimpse into the insecurities of the kidnappers and how their fragile ideology was leading them towards self-destruction. Khemlata recounts when one kidnapper asked them, *Do you want Pakistan or Hindustan?* Khemlata tactfully replied, *We are in Hindustan but if you want, then we can have neither Hindustan nor Pakistan, we can have azadi (independence)*. What else could she tell him to save her skin? In another instance, one dreaded Hizbul Mujahedeen terrorist on seeing her uncovered hands told her that in Islam, women's fingers should not be visible and tried to frighten them at gunpoint. With dialogues based on logic, tact, deep insight of their mindset and fearlessness (many times, they slapped the young boys when they behaved rudely), they won over the kidnappers. She says that they behaved with the kidnappers as parents would—using a combination of guidance and strictness whenever needed. Being in custody for 45 days, they witnessed death closely and eventually lost the fear of death. But deep inside, Khemlata felt that the kidnappers would not harm them and her belief became a reality when they were finally released.

During the peak of militancy in 1990, many Muslims were also threatened by the militants if they were found helping Indian supporters or informers, but many still helped the

Pandits find safe places. Pandits had no choice but to flee. This was the biggest churning and turmoil in the history of Jammu and Kashmir. Young Muslims were promised *azadi* by Pakistan who sold them dreams of a beautiful future and thought that just one *Allah Hu Akbar* cry would be enough to unite the Islamic world. On the other hand, Pandits fled from Kashmir thinking that the Government of India would support them and give them decent homes and jobs. However, this did not happen and both the communities were disillusioned. It dawned upon Pandits that they had to fend for themselves. The Wakhlus never left even after the traumatic kidnapping but a rumour was spread by the Pandits outside the valley that they had converted to Islam as they were perceived to be toeing the line of the local Muslims. However, Khemlata emphasises with pride that the Pandits who were left in Kashmir did maximum number of *hawans* (a Hindu ritual wherein offerings are made into a consecrated fire). All the Hindu shrines—Kheer Bhawani temple at Tulmul, Jyestha Devi temple, Kral Bab Ashram, Badrakali in Handwara and many others have been protected and new *ashrams* and *mandirs* (temples) have been constructed. Mamleshwar temple in Pahalgam is looked after by a Muslim, as there is no Hindu *pujari* (priest).

Khemlata has been conferred with many awards including a prize for a play called *Kashmir ki Dharti*, conferred by J&K Cultural Academy, and an award from Family Planning Association for conducting a drama on Family Planning. In the late eighties, taking a cue from the beginnings of unrest in the valley, she wrote a drama for Radio and Doordarshan (television) called *Lal Saeb*. It was a story of a Muslim man and a Hindu set against the backdrop of the fight for freedom. It was *abizet* (prophetic) because all hell broke loose in the nineties and thus began one of the most traumatic and horrific periods in the annals of Kashmiri history.

Khemlata has a message for all women. She says that women should be fearless and equal status will inevitably follow. According to her, women should be independent but maintain their traditions gracefully. She felt that having modern ideas is more important than wearing symbols of modernity like western dresses or knowing English. During her term as the Minister for Tourism in the J&K Government, or later as the Chairperson of the Central Social Welfare Board (J&K State), a cabinet rank post, she never felt discriminated and was always respected by everyone. She has never minced words, but has always maintained her grace and dignity. She was the only woman in a cabinet dominated by men, but did not view herself as the weaker sex. People were awed by her presence and character. She learnt to ignore rumours or discussions about her or her colleagues and continued to carry on her responsibilities with sincerity and dedication. She believes that when one is in tune with oneself and God, nobody can touch you. That is the source of her power and faith.

As a parting note about the return of Kashmiri Pandits to Kashmir, she says that they should keep their roots in the valley… after all it is their *janambhumi* (birthplace) and *janambhumi* is not always for permanent residence. She adds, "Anybody can go anywhere but roots have to be maintained. Stay for only four days but make your presence felt and keep your roots. There are so many religions and various denominations within Hindus, Muslims, Sikhs, Buddhists and Christians but we have to live like brothers and sisters if we want to progress. Like all living beings, we are all interdependent members of one global family".

Neerja Mattoo: A Symbol of Excellence in Education

Professor Neerja Mattoo was born in 1938 in Srinagar to Professor Shyam Lal Dhar who was a postgraduate from Lahore and a professor in SP College. Neerja has two brothers and two elder sisters. She taught English in the Government College for Women, Srinagar, for nearly four decades before retiring as the principal. She was awarded a British Council Visitorship to the University of Oxford. She has huge volume of work to her credit. She has translated three collections of Kashmiri short stories titled *The Stranger Beside Me*, *Contemporary Kashmiri Short Stories* and stories from Kashmir called *Kath* published by the Sahitya Akademi. She has translated works from Kashmiri to English of great Kashmiri writers like Amin Kamil, Akhtar Mohiudin, Ratan Lal Shant, Nazir Jahangir, Mustaq Ahmed Mustaq, Naeema Mahjoor and others. The latest addition to her repertoire includes the works of women poets like Arnimal and Habba Khatoon and spiritualists like Lal Ded and Rupa Bhawani (as part of the HRD Ministry Senior Fellowship in Literature for work on Kashmiri women poets). Possessing mastery over both English and Kashmiri, she has not allowed the nuances of Kashmiri to be lost in translation but has highlighted the beauty of Kashmiri through her eloquent translations. Being a multi-faceted personality, she has also authored two books on Kashmiri cooking—*The Best of Kashmiri cooking (*1975) and *Saal* (2008), and edited a book on Sharika Devi, a Shaiva *yogini* of Kashmir called *Shaktyollasah*.

Professor Neerja retired as Head of Department, English, and Principal of Women's College, MA Road in 1996. She is married with two sons. Her elder son, Aaditya, has a doctorate from Cambridge and works as a manager in the research wing of the World Bank while her younger son Amitabh, with a

DPhil from Oxford, is a professor in JNU and also Honorary CEO of Australia India Institute in Melbourne. At present he is a strategic analyst and advisor for education to the CM of Jammu and Kashmir. His family stays in Melbourne.

It was during the thirties that one girl ran away with her teacher (who also happened to be the student's cousin). This created such panic amongst Kashmiri Pandit parents that they withdrew their wards from schools. As a natural fallout, majority of the girls in the city (including Neerja's eldest sister) were tutored at home. This event set the social climate in those days but Neerja gives full credit to her father for his liberal outlook in those dark days. The fact that Neerja's elder sister graduated in 1954 and got admitted in Delhi School of Social Work for post-graduation speaks volumes about Prof Dhar's progressive ideas regarding women's education. She was sent to Delhi under the condition (put up by her mother) that she would return immediately if she received a marriage proposal. The inevitable happened—four or five months after Neerja's sister left for Delhi, she had to return to Srinagar to get married.

Neerja reminisces that she was tutored at home till the age of twelve and when her father was transferred to Jammu, she was admitted to a government school in Kachi Chhawani for the first time. Her father told the school to admit her in an appropriate class as per her level of proficiency. Fortunately, she was only tested in English, and as she was an avid reader, she passed the test easily. Those days, knowing a certain level of English was the benchmark of a good student. She was admitted to the 9th standard. She managed to do well in other subjects but failed in Mathematics. However, the family thought it was a mistake on the school's part. When her father returned to Srinagar, she was admitted in class 10 in a newly opened school called Kothi Bagh School, which was located in the premises of the Women's College. In those days, majority of the Pandit girls went to Vasanta School and some Muslim girls went to Mallinson Girls School.

When Women's College opened in 1950, Muslim girls were hardly visible in the college, but by late fifties there was a huge leap in their numbers. Not only girls from affluent families, even the have-nots started attending college. Some ambitious Pandit and Muslim girls from Neerja's class went to places like Patna, Amritsar and Delhi to pursue medicine and engineering as these courses were not offered in the state till then.

Speaking about her time in college, Neerja says:

> The year was 1952 and the college was only two years old when I entered it. Had it been founded earlier, my eldest sister, the brightest in the family, could also have gone to college after passing matriculation as a private student. She could not go beyond this step in her formal education because in 1941 there was only one college in Srinagar where her brothers went for higher education. The half a dozen girls on its rolls came from non-Kashmiri families—the 'advanced', 'modern' Punjabi girls, competing with whom was unthinkable for a 'respectable' Kashmiri Pandit girl. (Mattoo, Ref 17).

If proximity had a role to play then it worked well for Neerja. Her father's house was five to ten minutes walking distance from both Women's College and SP College: joining Women's College was an obvious option for her. After her graduation, she completed her postgraduation in English Literature from Jammu and Kashmir University. After completing her Masters, she had no idea that she would work. She happened to top in her MA and the Principal of the Women's College, Mehmuda

Ali, called her and advised her not to spend time in making *batta* (generic term in Kashmiri for cooking). She asked Neerja if she could take a class at the college as one of the teachers was on study leave. Her father was silent on hearing this proposal, but her mother was furious, commenting that no girl had gone out to work in their family. But Neerja was firm and her elder brother supported her decision. She felt that she could not say 'no' to Mehmuda who had taught her to have faith in herself. Her oft repeated lines echoed in every student's heart; "Always stand with a head held high and stand erect. Don't bow down!" Mehmuda's inspiring persona instilled confidence in her and proved to be a turning point in her life, encouraging her to join the teaching profession. She joined the college in 1958 and in 1967 became a full-time professor and head of the English department. Initially, her father thought that she would give up but she didn't because she simply loved her work. In fact, she continued working even after marriage.

The college developed close links with the British Council and UGC due to which the college held lot of workshops with well-known writers and poets.The Booker Prize winner Salman Rushdie visited Srinagar in 1983 and participated in a seminar on *Midnights Children* organised by the college. There was complete freedom at that time and Mehmuda Ali had created a climate for women's empowerment. Stalwarts like Begun Abdullah, Begum Zaffar Ali and Agha Ashraf (inspector of schools) greatly contributed to free thought and women's education. Mehmuda helped girls from humble backgrounds by providing books; she strategically increased their participation by encouraging them to go on study tours to heritage places in India like Ajanta and Ellora. She was truly a role model with secular and non-partisan views and impacted generations of girls. In her essay in the publication *Peace Kashmir,* Neerja recalls the golden period of education in Kashmir:

> Every eminent person from the world of politics, art, literature, music, economics or science, who came to Kashmir, would invariably be invited to the college to address the students or be introduced to the culture of Kashmir. These frequent encounters threw the windows wide open. If it was Jawaharlal Nehru one year, it could be Aneurin Bevan or Rajendra Prasad the next. The students who saw and heard Amartya Sen, Sardar Jafri, Begum Akhtar, or Stephen Spender in their college itself, did not need any more cosmopolitan exposure. The ease with which Kashmiri Muslim girls—most of them first generation literates—fitted into the routine of a modern college with its emphasis on sports, debating, NCC, educational tours and cultural activities is unimaginable in today's benighted state. No parent protested when their daughters were asked to participate in a march past with students from the two boys' colleges in Srinagar every month. Among them were married women, some of them mothers who were primary school teachers deputed to attend college and get a degree to improve their prospects. No voices were raised against the girls wearing the army-like NCC uniform or performing on the stage, reviving old Kashmiri folk song and dance forms, or travelling to places all over India in trains, the teachers roughing it out with them in second class compartments in order to learn about the history of India's past, without sermons being stuffed down their throats. Dramatics formed a very important part of our life in college.
>
> It was the rehearsal for a play we freshers saw when we ventured towards the little wooden hut-like structure that served as an auditorium in 1952 (The fully equipped large auditorium which we got from the government

in the 1960s after so many drama festivals—an annual feature—was burnt down in the 1990s). The play was about Habba Khatoon, who we learnt to our amazement had been a poet and consort of a king of Kashmir. This was our first introduction to the history of Kashmir, which till then was not taught at any stage of our school or college education. The dialogue was in English as the play had been written by a professor of the college who did not know Kashmiri, while the lyrics were Habra Keaton's own, set to music by the music department. That it was possible for our poor, disdained, till then looked-down-upon Kashmiri language to rub shoulders with the English language on equal terms was an overwhelming experience. This experiment, so new at that time, opened the doors to a whole world of mutually enriching linguistic and cultural cross currents.

Soon, we too became a part of this cultural revolution, eclectic in our choice of plays to act in, be they the poetic plays of Tagore (translated into English and Kashmiri), the farce-like comedies of Moliere in Urdu, the socially relevant satires of Ramesh Mehta in Hindustani, Bernard Shaw's witty exposes of social and political hypocrisies, the sparkling, epigrammatic Restoration comedies or the powerful human dramas of Shakespeare. And then we did something really extraordinary—we performed a folk opera celebrating a Kashmiri myth. It was the creation of two geniuses of modern Kashmir—the poet Dinanath Nadim and the music composer Mohanlal Aima. The attempt was so successful that it marked our entry into the first All-India Youth Festival held at Talkatora Garden in New Delhi in 1954. The cast included girls from orthodox families who had never ventured outside the valley of Kashmir, but such were the persuasive powers of the teachers and the principal that they were allowed to go, in the belief that whatever was part of the college activity

> must be good. The faith reposed by parents in their daughters by giving them the freedom to travel without a male relative as escort, was indicative of how much had changed within a short time.

Neerja emphasises that those days the sari was more of a cultural symbol than a religious one, and wearing a sari without covering the head was a sign of the secular and liberal climate of the state. In the early fifties, Mehmuda, followed by Shamla Mufti (another emancipated teacher educated in Aligarh who later became the principal of Nawakadal College) broke all norms by abandoning their *burqa.* They wore saris and did not cover their hair, inconceivable in today's time. When Neerja was studying, only some teachers would wear a *burqa* and take it off near the college. After some years, even that disappeared. By the end of the eighties, there has been a terrible downslide. Today, the literacy rate has increased in J&K but the quality of education has fallen. The social climate has deteriorated as most women are seen covered in *hijab* and have restricted mobility.

After 1990, nearly 3.5 lakh Kashmiri Pandits left the valley terrorised by the militants who had selectively killed members of this minority community. During this time, Neerja's sons were abroad and she along with her aged mother-in-law and husband decided to stay in the city as they felt quite safe, more so because they lived away from the city in Gogji Bagh. Neerja admits that if they had small school-going children, they probably would have shifted to Jammu or Delhi. However, one incident in 1991 shook them and they woke up to the fact that they were in the minority. Her husband was visiting the dentist when two gun-toting boys stopped his car and asked him to come with them. Mattoo tried to have a dialogue with them and explain that he was not a politician but they said that they wanted to take him to their headquarters. Realising the gravity of the situation, his private driver Abdul Ghani Dar tactfully took the militants to the side and tried to engage them in a conversation, giving Mattoo an opportunity to run to the neighbour's house and bolt the door from inside. Meanwhile, a police jeep came and the boys ran away.

When the news of the attempted kidnapping spread in the *mohalla*, people brought Mattoo back to his house in a procession, demonstrating solidarity and support. Fortunately, because of her husband's position (being Principal Chief Conservator of Forests), the government gave them security. Their employees and helpers, including their driver, *dhobi,* and gardener stood by them in those trying times. Following this incident, they sold their orchard at a pittance and people were expecting them to leave the city anytime. Recognising that a situation was created for them to leave, Mattoo decided that he would not leave his home as long as he could, maintaining a low profile throughout. Their sons would visit them regularly and were attached to Kashmir as they had lots of friends in the neighbourhood.

Post 1990, schools and colleges were targeted and carefully built-up libraries and laboratories went up in flames. In March of 1991, it was time to join the college but Neerja had no desire to do so. There were no Pandit girls in the college, and everyone else was dressed in black *abayas*. She felt like she was in a "futuristic horror movie" and decided to apply for leave. However, the principal of the college along with two other professors requested her to stay saying that the college could not function without her. In that year of crisis, Neerja took over as the new principal and continued to head the English department. She started by taking classes for new teachers who were facing a different work culture in a hostile environment. Hiding her inner trepidations, she faced the most exasperating and frustrating time of her career with a do-or-die attitude and courageously completed her term until she retired in 1996.

Elaborating on the gloomy climate that had set in, she says that militancy had begun to damage the psyche of people. The dress code and mobility of women was controlled. Movie theaters and video libraries were shut down. Saris were given up by teachers for *salwar kameez* and everyone started covering their head. The sari was viewed as Indian attire and was especially linked to Hinduism by Islamic extremists. Shamla Mufti (a former principal of the college) would counter the likes of Asiya Andrabi (head of the women's militant group *Dukhtaran-e-Millat*) and her grandniece by asking, "What are you doing? Don't you know the struggles we have gone through to achieve this freedom?" Imagining that she was voicing the sentiments of the young Kashmiri women of the valley, Asiya retorted by saying that she did not take advice from anybody who was over forty. Neerja says that prior to militancy when some women dressed up in *burqa* with only their eyes exposed, everybody would laugh at them. She adds that sudden radicalisation of the dress code took place in the nineties and almost everybody was wearing the *hijab*.

Though the youth of Kashmir are now well qualified with high expectations, the lack of jobs is giving rise to frustration and depression. Those belonging to elite families are not in the mainstream and their children are settled in other Indian states or abroad. Talking about peace building and building bridges, Neerja says that there is a climate of hatred for India. Young people have wavering views and lack conviction. On the other hand, Kashmiri Pandits who speak to the media have not lived in Kashmir but talk on behalf of the community including the miniscule minority in the valley. They are also full of hatred and living with malevolence. However, Neerja has learnt to survive in a depressing environment of mediocrity, bigoted and fanatical thinking by interacting with a few like-minded people who want to listen to sane voices. Writing and translating the rich oral and written literature of Kashmiris and inspiring the younger generation with the true nature of *Kashmiriyat* is her raison d'etre.

Vimla Dhar: Never Say Die

Dr Vimla Dhar, 78, was born in Srinagar to Triloki Nath Mattoo. Her mother was the only child of her parents. Vimla lost her mother at the age of six, a colossal loss for her as well as for her grandparents who raised her since her father was mostly travelling. She unhappily recalls that although she was encouraged to pursue her education like her brothers, they were sent to a better school like CMS (missionary school for boys) while she was admitted in the modest Vasanta School (non-missionary) since traditionally girls were not accorded the same status as boys in those days. When her grandfather had to move to Jammu, she left her school in Srinagar and was privately tutored in Jammu till the tenth standard. Her grandfather was keen that she become a Sanskrit scholar but she wanted to study medicine instead. She joined the Women's College in 1956 and opted for science subjects (hers was the 2nd or 3rd batch of science).Vimla calls it the golden period of her life. She joined MBBS in Prince of Wales Medical College, Patna, but during the third year of her course, her diabetic grandmother insisted that Vimla should get married before she died as she was keeping unwell.

Succumbing to emotional and societal pressure, Vimla grudgingly agreed and tied the knot with Dr SN Dhar, who later became a renowned physician in Srinagar. Unfortunately, her grandmother did not see the wedding and expired a month before the big day. By the time she completed her MBBS, she was seven months pregnant. Realising that it would be stressful for her to pursue gynaecology(her preferred branch) with her first baby, she became an assistant surgeon and later pursued post-graduation in pharmacology. Vimla has a son and a daughter who are married and settled in the United States. She took voluntary retirement as professor and head of pharmacology in 1998. Her husband, Dr SN Dhar expired in 2008 and at present she stays alone in her house in Rajbagh, Srinagar.

Vimla fidgets with an empty expression in her hazel eyes, concealing the deep anguish within as she recalls the harrowing nineties. In the wake of the targeted killings of Kashmiri Pandits and the threatening calls blared from the masjids, about three lakh Pandits fled the valley. In June 1990, she took leave for the forthcoming weddings of her children and went to Delhi; in August the same year, she got her son and daughter married. After the weddings, when she and her husband returned to Srinagar in September, everybody was surprised.

The year 1992 will be embedded in her memory forever as the most traumatic period of her life, when she was agonised both mentally and emotionally. In March 1992, her husband, Dr Dhar was abducted from his hospital by militants and kept in captivity for 83 days.

Two other non-Pandit professors from Regional Engineering College, Srinagar, and possibly from the University of Kashmir were also abducted along with him around that time. The militants wanted the top imprisoned militants to be released

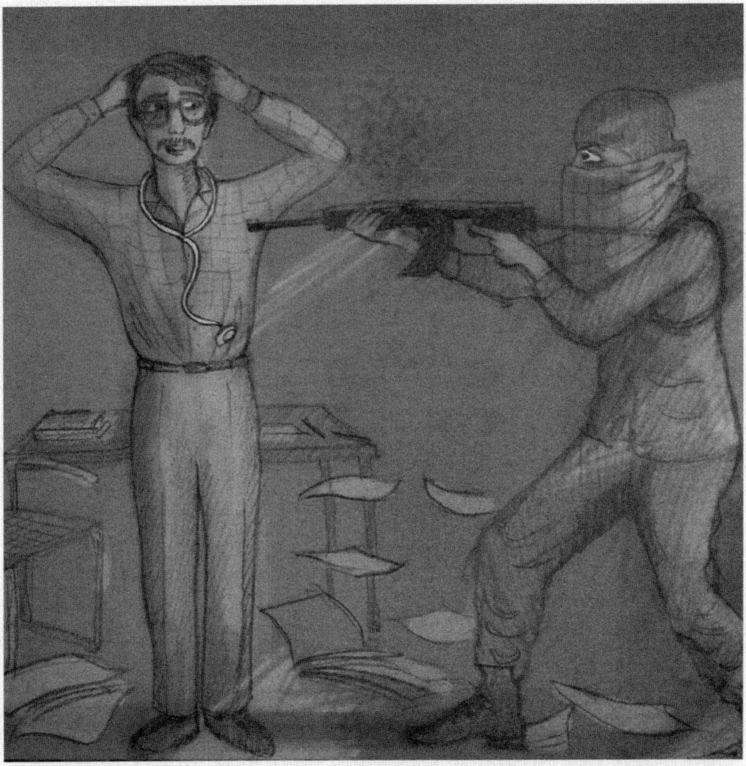

Dr SN Dhar was kidnapped in March 1992 and held in captivity for 83 days

in lieu of the hostages. Fearing a threat to their lives, Vimla's children and close relatives could not come to Kashmir to help her out during such a testing period of her life. Initially, there was no contact with the kidnappers and the police would come and ask her to identify unclaimed bodies in the mortuary. Every day, she would die a thousand deaths with new versions and updates being circulated about the location of the kidnappers and their demands. Reports like Dr Dhar has run away from captivity; his fingers have been chopped off and other gory details about his physical torture were doing the rounds. The reports were later found to be fabricated. Her relatives and government authorities advised her to leave the valley as she was risking her life, but misgivings about her husband's safety were causing her a lot of anxiety. Vimla decided to stay on in Srinagar.

She was advised to appeal to the government to release the militants. She did meet Saxena, the then governor, and requested him to ensure the safety of her husband. Exhibiting unparalleled strength of character and conviction, Vimla stood her ground. She says that what she had put forth to the governor was implemented. The authorities knew the locations of the kidnappers but did not attack them. The kidnappers were planning to take the hostages to Anantnag and to Dooru and ultimately to Simthan pass and then possibly cross over to Pakistan. It is in critical situations that human beings look for a redeemer or divine intervention. Although she was not particularly religious, somehow during this period Vimla drew strength from Shirdi Sai Baba. Every morning, she would cry before his image and felt that Sai Baba was communicating to her that her husband was safe. That gave her courage and writing notes in the evening about the day's events proved to be therapeutic. Her Muslim colleagues, friends and neighbours would visit shrines and *fakirs* to pray for her husband and provided her immense support. Dr Dhar's patients, some of whom would visit her almost daily gave her tremendous strength to face the ordeal.

Writing was perhaps therapeutic for Dr Dhar also. He wrote his horrendous experiences as a hostage during his 83-day captivity in his book *Eighty-Three Days–The Story of A Frozen River* published in 1992. After his release, he would talk light-heartedly about the treatment meted out to them saying that they got *dal pani* for lunch and *pani dal* for dinner. Lighter by 8 kgs when he was finally released by the kidnappers, Dr Dhar was welcomed by the whole neighborhood with flowers and *shireen* (tiny balls made of sugar) traditionally used in Kashmir for joyous occasions.

Commenting on the plight of Pandits, Vimla says that they suffered for no fault of theirs. In some weak moments she would often question their decision to stay back in Srinagar even after everyone else had left. Then she muses cheerlessly, "*Hamare liye aise bhi ujad gaya waise bhi ujad gaya*" (we have lost both ways), alluding to the situation of Pandits in Kashmir and outside in India. Although she has bad memories of Srinagar since the nineties, she is unable to erase the good memories that are associated with her place of birth. She still feels secure and at peace especially while tending to flowers in her beautiful garden. During the peak of militancy, when exodus from Kashmir was imminent for Pandits, the idea of leaving the flowers especially her favourite tulips would torment her. With tears in her eyes, she would talk to them saying "How can I leave you?"

Both she and Dr Dhar had ample opportunities to work in Delhi, but they came back. She says resignedly that the soil of Kashmir kept pulling her back and she does not regret it. But this beautiful valley did not deserve violence and bloodshed. In 1990, every night, sirens were blaring from fire brigades in the streets; houses were first looted and then burned to such an extent that militants did not leave behind anything. Bathroom fittings, plumbing material, tin roofs, taps and even coals from the burnt houses were sold. Humanity was at its lowest low. Remarking about the state of affairs in the valley during the past twenty-six years, she says, *"In China, they make wonderful things out of nothing and here we have reduced everything to nothing."*

Regarding the future of Kashmiri Pandits, she says that 99% are out of the valley and doing well for themselves.

Migration has to take place in order to generate revenue, especially in Kashmir where there are no job opportunities. She explains further, "But without a foothold, what is the future? America's population is made up of migrants from multi-ethnic backgrounds but they still look for their roots. Tomorrow our children will ask us about their roots and what will we tell them? Where will they go?" Her biggest regret is about the lack of state policy for sale of properties owned by Pandits post 1990. The government should have intervened and given the Pandit owners some amount (like five to ten lakh rupees) as security against their land. Their properties could be returned upon payment of this money when the situation improved. It would have made all the difference if the land was protected by the state, thus ensuring their return to Kashmir. Now how will they come back without a home? The situation has been totally mishandled and internationalised. As far as *azadi* is concerned, she asks, "How will Kashmir remain independent with Pakistan, China, Russia and Afghanistan as neighbours?"

Vimla's family also has a great legacy of philanthropic work started by her grandfather, Pandit Parmanand, who had opened Sharda Peeth Trust in his daughter's name in 1948. The trust activities included a regular school, an industrial center where sewing was taught to destitute girls and a research center focused on ancient Kashmiri culture. *Glimpses of Kashmiri Culture* and many other publications related to the heritage of Kashmir were produced till 1989. Dr Dhar was especially interested in preserving culture as many ancient historical names were being intentionally changed.

In 1970, the trust started a college but it did not get recognition as there was no place for expansion. After her grandfather passed away in 1970, Vimla took over as the president and introduced co-education in the school. Prior to militancy, there were almost 700 children enrolled with nominal fees. After 1990, most of the students left along with the staff and migrated to Jammu. The trustees have somehow managed to run the school with the help of some local teachers. However, all these efforts proved to be useless. On 8th May 1992, Sharada Peeth building was burned down by the militants and a treasure of publications was lost. It was also the period when Dr Dhar was abducted. Braving these stormy incidents of unimaginable shock and pain, Vimla continued to run the school with makeshift arrangements in a hall with 250 students. Loot and arson was the rule of those times. The remains of the burnt school building including the tin roof were stolen by one local militant. He promised to return it upon the reconstruction of the new school building but he was killed before the project took off. So, the hope of salvaging the roof was also buried with him. The new building was finally reconstructed but the school is perhaps on its last legs today as the roll is not even hundred. Vimla is toying with the idea of handing it over to the government but on the other hand, she wants to continue the vision initiated by her grandfather who was one of the pioneers of education for the underprivileged and research on ancient heritage. The other option is to shift it to some other locality as the present *mohalla* is known for harbouring militants, and the community has no value for education. She recalls that after 1990, they had struggled to call children from their homes to come to school.

Initially, she was very active with the peace initiatives started by Rajmohan Gandhi and participated in seminars in the US and Nepal. She would tell them the truth about the struggle for *azadi,* where even coals of burned houses were sold by cruel and merciless militants. Now she has withdrawn from everything. While relating her story, she says that she has spoken after many years, and in fact her children want her to document her experiences because they believe that she owes that to herself and future generations.

Depressed about the future of Kashmir, she says that some years ago there was still some hope, but at present the Islamic world is in total chaos and fundamentalist forces are ruling the world. Millions have been poured into Kashmir in the past twenty-six years and there are multiple lobbies with vested interests. In Saudi Arabia, they keep donation boxes for Kashmir's struggle for reinstating an Islamic caliphate.

Dr Vimla is now single-handedly battling with the repairs of her Rajbagh house that was submerged in water after the floods in 2014.

Girija Dhar: A Role Model of Syncretic Culture

Meeting Dr Girija Dhar was a long cherished dream for me. She is a phenomenal woman who defied all societal conventions by having an interfaith marriage, an unthinkable prospect in the early sixties. She was married to Late Dr Nasser Ahmed (who passed away recently), a renowned physician, Padma Shree awardee, former principal of Government Medical College and former member of Legislative Council, Srinagar. They have a daughter, Dr Tina Anjila Shah who lives in USA with her husband Dr Anil Koul.

While asking the inevitable question about the reaction to her interfaith marriage, she unwaveringly stated that she never faced any opposition or hostility from her family or her husband's family. Although her mother was deeply hurt by this alliance, she exhibited remarkable equanimity, accepting their marriage gracefully and instructed her other daughters to desist from discussing Dr Girija's marriage. Dr Nasser belonged to a highly educated and a progressive family. His two sisters Mehmuda Ahmad Ali Shah and Rehana Jalaluddin were great educationists.

Recalling her early childhood, Girija said that her elder sister was allowed to open a school in Gogji Bagh in Srinagar, but her second sister who wanted to become a doctor faced stiff opposition from the family. By the time Girija grew up, the mindset in the family had changed considerably and she pursued her education smoothly, unopposed.

Soon after completing her college education in Sri Pratap College, which was primarily a boys' college since Women's College did not have a science stream till then, she went to KGMC (Kasturba Gandhi Medical College), Lucknow in 1956 for her MBBS followed by DRCOG (Diploma of the Royal College of Obstetricians and Gynaecologists) at London in 1962 and FRCS (Edinburgh) in 1964. She joined the department of Obstetrics and Gynaecology at Government Medical College, Srinagar in 1964 as Assistant Professor and then served as Head of the Department till 1985. She was the Dean and Principal of Government Medical College, Srinagar till her retirement in 1992. After her retirement, she became a member of the State Public Service Commission (PSC) for three years. Thereafter, she became the Chairperson of Social Welfare Advisory Board for one year and was elevated to Chairperson, State Commission for Women. An extremely polished and poised woman, Dr Girija was instrumental in running the gynaecological and obstetrics services in the valley. Apart from being an excellent teacher and clinician, she is known to have made great strides in the reduction of maternal mortality in the valley due to her technical and management skills. She was also instrumental in opening the 500-bed Lal Ded Maternity Hospital in Srinagar.

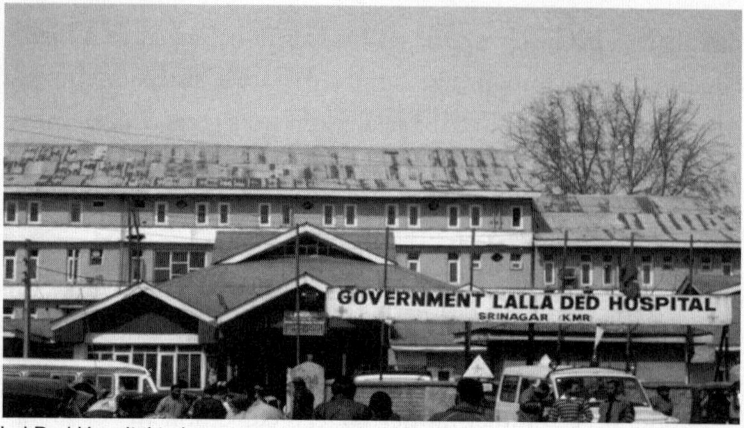

Lal Ded Hospital today

After her marriage to Dr Nasser, she found that they (she and her husband) were respected equally by Muslims and Hindus primarily because they were doctors. Their bond was based on their common worldview of a secular, tolerant and pluralistic society where all faiths were allowed to flourish.

After 1990, Dr Girija lent support to predominantly Pandit schools like Vasanta and Kashyapa (managed by Women's Welfare Trust) which were in shambles after the exodus of students as well as teachers. The schools were crying for help as they were badly damaged during militancy. She collected donations from various sources to renovate the schools. One of her donors, Rama Vaidyanathan, a talented Bharatanatyam dancer performed free for the Trust in June 2012 at SKICC Auditorium, Srinagar. This three-part dance presentation called *Kashmir, Kashmiris and Kashmiri* was based on Lal Ded's poetry narrated by Ms Meera Khanna, a writer and a social activist. The collections received through the sale of tickets were used for the renovation work of the schools and for training teachers. They also received donations from the then Governor NN Vohra. Girija also sent students for training to Bharti Airtel through her contacts with the CEO but due to some differences with other trustees on the board, she stepped down from the trusteeship of the board. She has also been a crusader for women's rights in the valley, be it discrimination in education or the legal status of Kashmiri women who get married to non-state subjects. She is also the Chairperson of Rahat Ghar, a unique shelter home for widows and children affected by conflict. It was initiated in 2000 and is presently located in Chandilora, Tangmarg. The objective is to provide a safe environment and rebuild the lives of these women and children by imparting education and vocational skills. It is managed by the Guild For Services and supported by the Department of Women and Child Development, Government of India.

Girija was of the opinion that Kashmir could not be part of Pakistan and *azadi* was not possible. She believed that people did not really understand the different facets of autonomy. Most well-to-do young Kashmiri Muslims have migrated to countries like Saudi Arabia, Dubai, UK and USA, leaving the parents to face the political conflict here. On the other hand, economically backward youth do not have anything to look forward to, as there are no government jobs and industries in the state anymore. Tourism is the main source of income for the local people, and over the past twenty-seven years, that has been impacted the most.

While talking about Kashmiri Pandits, she said that it was good that they migrated and prospered outside. She remarked, "Here in the valley, they were struggling to get government jobs. It is unfortunate that Pandits, who had a choice of not selling their properties, did so. Now, they should buy property here. Many of them have already started doing that. If not for permanent settlement, they should come to their homeland as tourists. Why should they leave such a beautiful place and go anywhere else?"

She faced threats and was personally attacked during militancy but that did not prevent her from staying on in the valley. She said that all her relatives asked them to move out but she did not budge. Her Pandit colleagues in the medical college were threatened with their names written on the board. She told them to take leave and go to Jammu. She felt she hade made a wise decision because failure to ensure their safety would have weighed heavily on her. Apart from her contribution in reviving the Vasanta and Kashyapa schools, her biggest role has been staying put in Srinagar and facing the situation bravely, thus upholding the secular traditions of the valley. Unfortunately, Dr Girija expired in 2018 becoming a legendary figure symbolising compassion, perseverance and belief in innate human goodness that transcended barriers of religion and caste.

Peace Initiatives in the Valley

The Peacemakers

Before embarking upon the initiatives made by the 'Peacemakers' or 'Rebuilders', I want to dwell on the formal peace building processes in the valley over the past three decades. Does peace education help in changing the mindset? What involves reconstruction? Fathers and mothers are a child's first teachers and they nurture peace in the family. This peace is enhanced at school. Peace is a broad concept with practical and spiritual connotations. It can imply a state of inner calm or end of conflict. Peace has been understood to mean the absence of conflict or violence and conversely as the presence of harmony, accord, security and understanding in society.

Concept of Peace Education

Peace education is planning a strategy of eliminating the conflicts and violence caused by injustice, inequality and human rights violations and implementing the ways and means of reducing these through appropriate teaching and learning tactics for producing responsible global citizens to spread peace in the world. Therefore, peace education should be one of the goals of education.

There is no universally accepted definition for Peace Education. A good number of definitions are available on the basis of different perceptions and approaches. Webster defines peace as a "state of quiet or tranquility, freedom from disturbance or agitation, calm repose".

Betty Reardon, (famous peace educationist) defines Peace Education as the "attempt to promote the development of an authentic planetary consciousness that will enable us to function as global citizens and to transform the present human condition by changing the social structures and patterns of thought that have created it".

According to John Dewey (proponent of social change and education reform), "Peace education is grounded in active citizenship, preparing learners for assiduous participation in a democracy, through problem posing and problem–solving education, and a commitment to transformative action in our societies".

Betty Reardon also makes a reference to the concept of positive peace and negative peace. According to her, the term negative peace refers to an absence of war, physical or direct violence while the term positive peace is used to refer to the presence of non-exploitative relationships or conditions of social and economic justice. She, therefore, recognises that the problem of concern for peace educators are manifold, including diverse areas such as economic deprivation, development, environment, resources, and universal human rights and social justice. Reardon's concept of peace is supported by many educationists (SH Toh and Virginia Floresca—Cawagas et al). According to these educationists, peace education covers diverse issues. The aim of peace education is perhaps best summarised in the Hague Appeal for peace which states that a culture of peace will be achieved when citizens of the world: a) Understand global problems, b) Have the skills to resolve conflicts constructively, c) Know and live by international standards of human rights, gender and racial equality, d) And appreciate cultural diversity and e) Respect the resources of the earth.

From these definitions it is understood that peace education inculcates the higher order of human values and aims at the overall development of individuals (Source: Centre For Distance Education and Peace Education, Bharathidasan University, Tiruchirapalli).

The following paragraphs delve into the initiatives taken till date in the Valley:

Initiatives by Centre for Dialogue and Reconciliation

The Centre for Dialogue and Reconciliation (CDR) aims to be a catalyst for peace in South Asia. It strives to do this through a process of dialogue and discourse, achieving peaceful settlements of conflicts with justice and equality. Its overall mission and eventual goal is to facilitate reconciliation between adversaries in South Asia. CDR has done sustained work in Jammu-Kashmir for 15 years and helped towards building peace infrastructure in that state. Throughout 2004, the Intra-Regional Dialogues evolved to become a series of Intra-Kashmir dialogues. In 2005, these brought together a significant number of people across the border, well ahead of the governmental process. As an outcome of these dialogues, a clear consensus emerged across the political spectrum regarding several important issues. Topics included:

- The rejection of violence as a tool to resolve the conflict
- The need for an inclusive dialogue process
- The need for a solution applicable to all three regions and acceptable to all three parties
- The importance of Kashmiris deciding their own future
- Ceasefire and return of refugees and arrangements for those stranded across the line of control
- An end to human rights violations and a reduction of security forces in civilian areas

Not only was the information and dialogue outcome shared with civil society through several write-ups in local newspapers, but the resolutions were also brought to the attention of policy makers in the government. Some of the issues and concerns raised during the dialogues were widely circulated and discussed by concerned people in the government. These are also published in the book called *Beyond Borders.* In some instances, CDR has been instrumental in shaping government policies to answer specific needs and aspirations of the people. The policy change has been reflected in several governmental initiatives, including suggestions for opening travel and trade routes in all three regions of Azad Kashmir (AJK), Pakistan and Jammu & Kashmir. Since 2005, CDR has organised over sixteen "Cross-LoC (Line of Control) Dialogues" and is the only organisation to do so in Jammu&Kashmir.

Aside from the above, CDR took initiatives to create training material for peace education. For four years, training programmes were held in J&K where hundreds of teachers were taught the concepts of peace education. In 2004, some of the women involved in this process suggested that something ought to be done to facilitate a meeting between them and their counterparts on the other side of the LoC.

The Conference

Finally, after many stumbling blocks, the first Intra-Kashmir Women's Conference—Connecting Women Across the Line of Control—was held in Srinagar from November 16-18, 2007, organised by the Centre for Dialogue and Reconciliation (CDR) in collaboration with the Women's Studies Centres of the universities of Kashmir and Jammu. The conference was historic in more ways than one. It was the first time that women from both sides of the Line of Control (LoC) were able to meet. It was held in Srinagar and the delegation from Azad Jammu Kashmir (AJK) travelled to India via the Wagah border. It took place in an atmosphere that allowed delegates to speak freely and frankly and express differences as well as areas of agreement. For many of the twelve women from Pakistan and AJK who travelled via Wagah and through Jammu to Srinagar, it was the first time they had visited areas in Jammu & Kashmir that lay on the other side of the border.

The delegation was diverse and included a human rights activist, an academician, a woman entrepreneur, a doctor, lawyers, a grassroots women's organiser, a former Director of Women's Education and a television journalist. It excluded women who are involved in power politics or are the predictable participants of international meetings. The delegates from

J&K comprised of writers, educationists, a former Chairperson of the J&K State Women's Commission, college principals, directors of women's studies centers of universities and colleges, journalists, doctors, television anchors, advocates and women activists.

CDR organised seven Intra-Kashmir gatherings between 2005 and 2007. These ran parallel to the official peace process between the Governments of India and Pakistan and resulted in creating an informal network of individuals interested in the peace process on both sides of the LoC. The wide-ranging discussions in these conferences helped to build a wider peace constituency on both sides. However, despite all the efforts made by CDR, women's participation in these Intra-Kashmir gatherings was not adequate and nothing concrete emerged from these dialogues.

The Rebuilders

Promoting qualities of tolerance, understanding, cooperation and respect for the differences in others is a strategy which can be adopted by the educational system. There is a need to transform the conditions in society by changing the social structures and patterns of thought that have created conflicts through problem solving education. At another level, tackling poor economic development, mental and physical health, and saving environment and resources can be an active way of promoting peace and development in the valley.

It is with this spirit of documenting the peace and rebuilding initiatives that the following interviews were conducted to understand the true essence of peace and reconstruction. Attempts made by educationists, NGOs, environmentalists, preservers and promoters of literature and art and sports in the state are actually paving the way for changes. By using their skill sets to identify and deal with problems constructively, they have carved a path or a blueprint of what should comprise a peaceful, progressive and stable society. In the interviews some individuals have expressed frustration, despair and pessimism, while others are hopeful for a brighter future and take pride in small victories in shaping the future of the valley.

Nusrat Andrabi: A Peace Educationist

Professor Nusrat Andrabi was born in 1945 in Srinagar. Her father served the police as DIG and although her mother was just a matriculate, she encouraged Nusrat to pursue her studies. Nusrat graduated in Arts from J&K University and did her postgraduation in Urdu. She completed her MPhil and PhD from Iqbal Institute in Kashmir between 1981 and 1984. Her doctoral thesis was on comparative study of Urdu writers and poets like Haali, Akbar Illahabadi, Iqbal and Ali Ahmed Suroor. She served in three women's colleges in the state—at Iqbal Institute for 28 years, as principal of Women's Colleges at Baramulla (2000) and Maulana Azad Road, Srinagar (2000–2003). She is the wife of late Professor Mohammad Amin Andrabi, who was a renowned scholar and academician. Nusrat has been a member of Jammu & Kashmir State Waqf Board and is presently the honorary secretary of Red Cross Society. She has written several articles on women's issues.

She has been witness to the decline in education during militancy and has made immense efforts to maintain the quality and standard of higher education. According to her, education was most impacted during the period of militancy—a period when all the students suffered due to shutdowns, curfews, searches and crackdowns. Schools were torched and laboratories in higher secondary schools were destroyed. During 1990-92, there was mass copying during exams, but she says that the education department was still able to prevent at least 70% of the students from doing so.

Today, government schools including reputed schools like Vishwa Bharati, DAV, Jawahar Nagar, and National School are on the verge of extinction while private schools have proliferated in huge numbers. Khalsa and Lal Ded School have closed down. Ten teachers are appointed with just two students in government schools, and like elsewhere in the country, coaching classes have mushroomed everywhere with students bunking school to attend these classes.

Recalling the horrific period of militancy, she says that there were nearly a hundred blasts outside the Women's College, one of which caused the death of a young girl. Notwithstanding the climate of fear and uncertainty, parents made sure that their wards went to college. Barring the first fortnight, the college remained open during peak militancy period and students from Nawakadal College shifted to Women's College for a year and a half. According to Nusrat, the best institutions were reduced to the worst state. Many teachers went to Jammu, especially those who feared for their lives due to militancy. Today, nearly eighty percent of the staff is contractual and only twenty percent are permanent, leaving the contractual staff disheartened and devoid of any commitment towards their work. In an attempt to bring back normalcy and save students from losing their precious years, the Government of India announced the need for new colleges and the state jumped at this opportunity without providing any infrastructure and staff.

Fear has been the key to everything that has happened post 1990. When Pandits left the valley, the majority community of Muslims did not stop them. The targeted killings of Pandits gave rise to fear psychosis which led to their mass exodus. Nusrat recalls that at that time, an unruly student sent letters to Bakshi, a Pandit teacher in Burn Hall School, in which he threatened to kill him if he did not leave the Valley. Then he sent another letter in which he wrote, "If you don't leave in two days, they (militants) will kill you". So, Bakshi had no choice but to leave. It is not only the Pandits who left the valley—about 2.5 lakh Muslims also followed suit. So many of Nusrat's relatives in Mattan left for Jammu and have now built houses in Sidra. In 1989, one family with a carpet business was asked for a heavy price by the militants. They were even asked to hand over their son for training. They paid some amount and left for Delhi ; now they only visit Srinagar for family functions.

Regarding the changes in the racial/religious demography of the state, Nusrat says that in 1988, her son had only Pandit friends but her younger daughter does not know a single Pandit. Children in the valley have not seen Hindu festivals post 1990. She adds disparagingly that Pandits saved themselves, but the Muslims who were left behind are affected by mental diseases. For 27 years now, people have been living with uncertainty and fear at every step, giving rise to high stress levels. According to her, about fifty percent of the population is silently suffering from depression. Since the past twenty years, parents continue to enquire whether the schools are open. Bombs, disruptions or cross firing between terrorists and police/army are a daily worry. It was a common practice of security forces to conduct sudden searches, stopping buses and ordering people to alight from the buses and walk. They would not even spare girl students. She adds that now they have become used to 5-6 days of curfew in a month. People have lost their freedom of speech—they do not know what to say and to whom. Men in general have become aggressive and villagers fear death if they do not come out to condone the death of a militant.

There is nothing productive happening as there is no work culture. There is frustration and hopelessness amongst the youth as there are no jobs even after getting professional degrees. Such youth easily fall prey to militant activities. About one lakh people have died and their family members are seething to avenge the death of their slain relatives. Nusrat says that Kashmir is a 'divorced couple *ka bacha*' (child of divorced parents), the parents being India and Pakistan. If the plebiscite had happened during Sheikh Abdullah's time in 1955, the disease would not have become so serious and uncontainable.

As if militancy was not enough to devastate the state, the floods in 2014 worsened the condition of the best educational institutions like Amar Singh College, J&K Cultural Academy, Sri Pratap Museum and library, Presentation Convent, Burn Hall School, Bemina College, SP College library and laboratories. Treasures like books, photographs and records of fifty-three years of Women's College were totally washed out. While narrating the aftermath of the floods, Nusrat regretfully says that even her personal diaries were lost.

While talking about the impact of militancy on the people of the state, she holds the Arab and Jamaat-e-Islami culture responsible for the introduction of *abayas* (an Arabic form of *burqa*) in the valley. She says that during the height of militancy, hardly ten percent of women could be seen wearing the *burqa*, now almost eighty percent are wearing it. She recollects that one very progressive family regressed as their two sons joined the Jamaat-e-Islami and all the women in the family started wearing the *burqa*. She however clarifies, "I never wore the *burqa*, nobody told me to do so. I told my husband that the day they tell me to wear a *burqa*, I will stop going to college."

According to her, Kashmiris will not accept this diktat for long because they like changes, alluding to the fickle temperament of the people and the weather. Fearing the *wahabis* (an Arabic Islamic sect that does not believe in saints and Sufis but only one Allah), people did not visit Maqdoom Sahib (a Sufi shrine) earlier but now they have restarted the practice. According to her, the outpouring of religious channels (Islamic as well as Hindu) on television and the internet have negatively influenced young minds in the last decade or so.

She has been actively involved in peace initiatives with Centre for Dialogue and Reconciliation started by Rajmohan Gandhi along with Sushobha Barve and other like-minded individuals. They had formed a policy group, and a delegation of ten women from Azad Kashmir and others from Jammu and Kashmir attended the peace conference held in Srinagar in 2007. However, as women members, the group realised that they had no political voice and no real representation of the political parties and separatist groups in the state. Hurriyat has no women members and during the fight for *azadi* (Independence), women were never consulted.

Tracing the improvement in women's status and political involvement historically, she says that in the last 70-80 years, Begum Abdullah (Sheikh Abdullah's wife) and GM Sadiq's (erstwhile Chief Minister of Kashmir) sister tried to improve the status of women but nothing much could be achieved. As the standard of living has improved, some women (especially those with the right connections) are supplementing the family income. But there is a constant fear lurking in these women. Today, we have women doctors, engineers, professors, senior judges, senior police officers, teachers and IAS (Indian Administrative Service) officers in the state but there is no political involvement. Women are still on the margins. Reflecting on the historical situation of women, Nusrat emphasises that women rulers have never been treated well, be it Razia Sultana in Delhi or Kota Rani in Kashmir. Women like Lal Ded, Rupa Bhawani and Habba Khatoon were also ill-treated by their families.

She and her team have made efforts to explain the peace process by using peace books but they have not yielded any positive response from the students or the J&K Education Board. She also tried to advocate for inclusion of Peace Education in the school curriculum, but the Board thought that it would unnecessarily burden the students as well as the teachers. Disappointed, Nusrat says that NGOs involved in peace initiatives have not been successful in the state.

However, on a positive note, she observes that despite Hurriyat's attempts to clamp down on the opportunities given to women for their growth and self-expression, subtle changes like restarting the Music College and opening of the Department of Journalism and Mass Communication in the university have opened doors for the young generation of girls and boys. The youth now have an opportunity to think independently. Girls especially are writing, reporting and giving a voice to the otherwise voiceless half of the state. These youth, she believes, are the only hope for the future.

Vijay Dhar: Sowing the Seeds of Reason and Peace through Education

The Delhi Public School, Srinagar, is the first private school affiliated to the Central Board of Secondary Education (CBSE). The school was set up by the DP Dhar Memorial

Trust in the name of Late Durga Prasad Dhar, a public figure of great eminence. He unfortunately died at the peak of his public service career on 12th June 1975, when he was only 56 years of age. Late Shri Dhar held various ministerial appointments in the state of Jammu & Kashmir and the union cabinet. He was known for his philanthropy, his dedication to the people of Jammu & Kashmir state and above all for his untiring efforts and total commitment to the cause of integration of J&K with the rest of India. He was of the firm belief that the best way to integrate the state of Jammu & Kashmir with the rest of the country was to strengthen the socio–economic fabric of the state by making the people of Kashmir self-reliant, industrious and proud of their 'Kashmiriyat'. It is against this backdrop that he envisioned education as an essential instrument to achieve these goals.

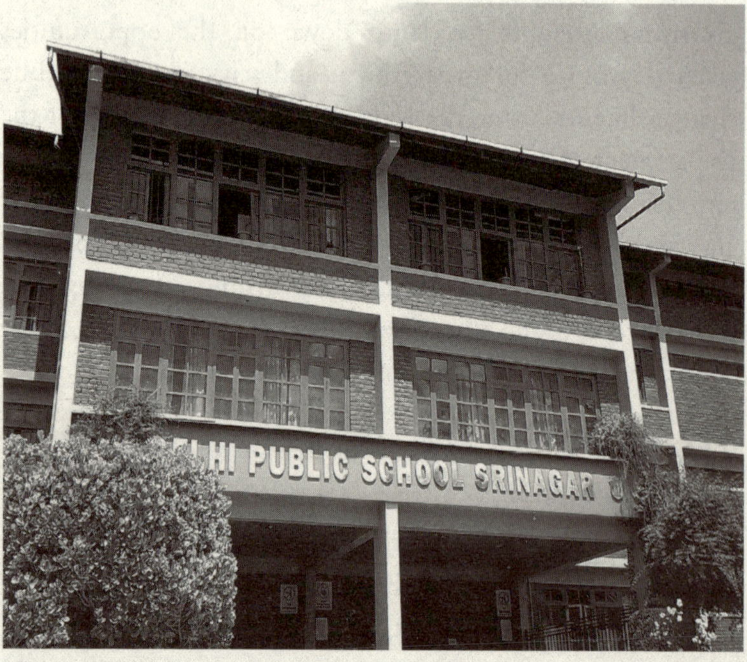

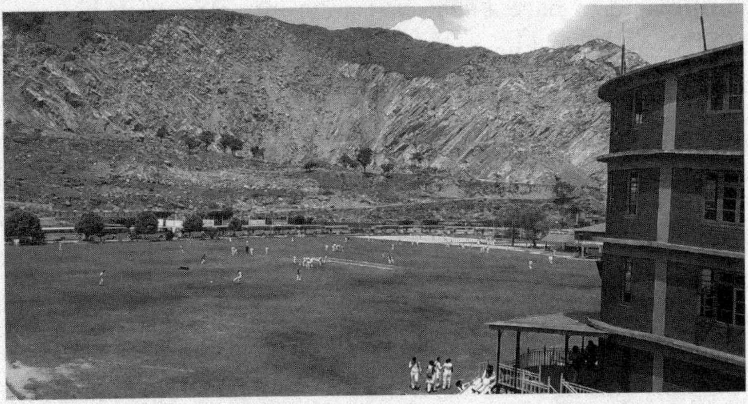

Delhi Public School, Srinagar (2017)

Vijay is the son of Late Durga Prasad Dhar. He studied at Jamia Millia Islamia, Delhi, and went to Chennai to study engineering but later migrated to Regional Engineering College, Srinagar, to complete the course. He has remained active in politics and social life. To honour the memory of his late father and to complete the unfinished task left by him, Vijay Dhar fulfilled his father's dream by constituting a public trust where family members contributed the initial corpus. Started on 10th March 2003, amidst the backdrop of beautiful mountains on sprawling fifteen acres of land, Delhi Public School Srinagar has been an agent of change in the conflict-ridden state and a beacon of hope to the otherwise despondent and hapless children. The school has two libraries—the senior section has 50,000 and the junior one has 17,000 books. They also have a separate section for Kashmiri books. It also has a yoga centre and a canteen. The nursery block is painted in vibrant colours and the creativity of children is encouraged through various workshops.

As I enter the cozy and homely office of Vijay Dhar, Director DPS, I am struck by his informality and warmth. I am invited to have a chat over a cup of coffee with him and Ms Kusum Warikhoo, the outgoing principal who has served the school for six years. At the time of my interview (May 2017) she had just retired. Vijay is humble and quiet, and deserves a medal of bravery for the infrastructure that he has created in the past fourteen years amidst tumultuous conditions in the Valley. According to Vijay, Kashmiris realised the importance of education after 1951 when Sheikh Mohammad Abdullah declared education compulsory. He feels that education got a big fillip during the time of Bakshi Ghulam Mohammad who set up medical, engineering and teachers training colleges and tied up with Aligarh Muslim University. At that time, if one did an MA from Aligarh University, one got an LLB degree free. Two seats were reserved for Kashmiris in each technical college of India. However, this practice stopped in 1977.

Talking about the horrendous 1990s, Vijay says that like all Pandits they too left the city in 1990, but by 1992, his mother had started pining for her homeland. They came back with heavy security and gradually settled down.

Prior to 1990, Pandits dominated the education scene and suddenly after their exodus, there was a huge vacuum. In 1992-93, more than 1 lakh Muslim boys and girls went out of the state and sought admission in colleges there. Looking at the dismal state of affairs, Vijay thought of what his father, the late Durga Prasad would have wished for the state—a world-class educational institution. So, the seed was sown in 1996-97, but it took another year to convince DPS to come to Srinagar (they were operating in Jammu), and a year for the CBSE syllabus to be accepted. Finally, Delhi Public School came into fruition in 2003. The response from parents was phenomenal despite the fact that it was the first CBSE and a co-educational school, an idea that was socially unacceptable at the time.

On asking why a Pandit would be interested in opening a school for Muslims when the entire Pandit community had been hounded out of the valley, Vijay responds by saying that it was the need of the time. Adding to his response, Kusum Warikhoo says that when she was approached to run DPS in Srinagar, she willingly accepted the challenge because she wanted to give something back to the Valley. She was born, bred and educated in Kashmir and even worked in the city in a multi-cultural era where religion or caste was irrelevant. Echoing the same sentiment, Vijay continued talking about his apprehensions about the success of his venture, which were finally put to rest by the encouragement he received from parents and friends.

Given the years of conflict in the valley, parents were very keen to impart good education to their children. In one case, a mother who found the school fees exorbitant (Rs 1200 per month at that time) decided not to admit her child in the school. But she came back after a few days saying *"Main chawal kam karoongi, tel kam karoongi, par mere bachhe ko yahin padhaongi).* (I will have less rice; use less oil but I will educate my child here).

It appears that the school authorities had to deal with a lot of challenges which they and the children faced on a daily basis. Initially, introduction of co-education elicited responses like "Boys should be admitted to DPS and girls to convent schools" and "Children get spoilt here". Today 60% of the students are boys and 40% are girls. Now parents are more open and accepting of the idea of co-education.

Delhi Public School has been working on changing the mindset and exposing the students to diverse cultures, ideologies while encouraging debates and free thinking. For example, they have now appointed a new principal, Mr Balasubramanium, who comes from South India. Vijay and Kusum say that they have been able to open students' minds by introducing them to music, literature, history and books of Kashmiri folklore. Kusum remarks, "We do not brush contentious issues aside, but we let them think and reason. We take them for visits to temples like Kheer Bhawani and to gurdwaras and let them witness Eid, Gurupurab and Diwali celebrations in the school."

In 2010, schools were closed for five months and children were sent to Delhi. The authorities had thought that only 10-15 students would be ready to go to Delhi but to their astonishment, they were saddled with 110 children and teachers who spent two months in the capital till they finished their examinations. In the same year, children from 9th and 10th standards did not attend school for six months. Teachers were sent to their homes and nodal schools were created. Today, children come to DPS from all over the valley—Baramulla, Anantnag and Rajouri, Verinag, Kulgam, Magam and Sumbal. They have 14 buses to Pulwama ferrying 400-500 children every day. Today, the school has made inroads into the homes of children. If a child is absent or faces some family problem, students and teachers promptly visit them and try to offer help. In that way, the school is an extended family.

Engaging children in music festivals and sports is the key to attain a healthy psyche. DPS held an inter-school Kashmiri music competition in 2015 where 9,000 children from various schools of the valley participated and an equal number of people came to listen to them. Another major event was the Under-17cricket tournament. Ten to fifteen teams comprising of 4,800 children participated in the event.

The state curriculum has nothing on Kashmir's past legacy and history but DPS is making a deliberate attempt to write booklets based on the rich cultural and social history of Kashmir. Children read a lot and correct teachers if they cite incorrect historical facts. In addition to the rich collection of history and literature books, the paintings in the library highlight the contribution of various historical personalities, be it Hindus, Buddhists, Muslims or Sikhs. Both Vijay and Kusum say that they have sowed the seeds of reasoning amongst these children who are growing up in the most depressing and challenging time in the history of Kashmir.

Despite dark clouds of gloom in the valley, there is a silver lining at the end. What is heartening to note is that children who pass out from DPS are doing very well wherever they go. Some are in Jamia Millia, JNU, or in engineering and medical colleges. In the early years of the school, parents were reluctant to send girls outside the state but now that is changing drastically. Girls seek admission in colleges like Lady Shri Ram and St Stephens in Delhi and even in colleges located in Bangalore and Pune. Some of the students have become astrophysicists and art choreographers in the United States. All these achievements demonstrate that Vijay is on the right track. He quietly smiles with satisfaction as he witnesses a period where parents and children are choosing education, progress and peace as against conflict and strife.

Gurmeet Singh: Weaving Gender Studies with Formal Education

Born in Srinagar, Gurmeet is the young face of the new generation of Kashmiri educationists. Schooled in Mallinson and Arya Samaj Schools, Gurmeet graduated in science and was offered postgraduation in biochemistry. Since the department had limited seats, she changed her stream and enrolled for postgraduation in English Literature. She later completed her B Ed from Government College of Education on MA Road, now rechristened as Institute of Advanced Studies in Education (IASE), Srinagar. Gurmeet is also a singer and has conducted many radio programs. She lives with her two married brothers in Srinagar.

After the events of 1990, educational establishments were shut for a month and a half and everything was paralysed marked by uncertainty and hopelessness. She says that Kashmiri Pandits and Sikhs were killed and were given life-threatening notices to leave the valley. Pandits left en-masse but Sikhs were in a quandary about their future. Gurmeet's father, Prem Singh, who was a professor and a leader of the Sikh community stepped in and advised them against following the path of the Pandits. He reasoned that Pandits could fend for themselves as they were well educated, but with limited skills and low education, Sikhs had no future outside. He questioned his community members, "Why should we leave our space?" He along with other senior leaders had a dialogue with the leaders of the Azadi movement and asked them to protect their community. And that was the point of no return.

Gurmeet started her career with adhoc jobs in some government and private schools. She taught methodology of teaching, focusing on teachers' training at Degree College, Tral, Pulwama district, Kashmir. In 2004, as per NAAC (National Assessment and Accreditation Council) recommendation, the Women's Studies Centre was opened in 2006 in the College of Education with the objective of emancipating women by building their confidence. They wanted to enable the economic, social, cultural, political and mental empowerment of women and increase their awareness about their rights, health and hygiene. Through outreach activities like workshops, research studies and dissemination via publications, the center has been making strides in bringing young girls to the forefront. Currently, Parveen Pandit is the principal of the College of Education, Srinagar, and director at the Women's Studies Centre, while Gurmeet is the coordinator.

In the early days of the establishment of Women's Studies Centre, Gurmeet conducted programs on adolescent health, reproductive changes and hygiene for students. In the second phase, since 2011, the center is conducting SAM (Sensitivity Awareness for Managers) training in higher education for women as well as capacity building programs. They have produced a manual for leadership development, communication skills and so on. Till date, they have conducted two residential SAM programs. They have five–six regular research scholars and some part-time researchers as well.

The center has held many workshops like 'Gender Violence and Rights of Women', 'Management of Adolescent Problems through Counselling Strategies' and 'Legal Education for Women' in collaboration with WISCOMP (Women in Security Conflict Management and Peace). Some research studies have pertinent topics like *Violence Against Women in Kashmir*, *Review of Science Curriculum at Secondary Level from Gender Perspective*, *Women's Empowerment in Kashmir* and *Gender Bias in Languages* to name a few.

In November 2007, the center, in collaboration with Centre for Dialogue and Reconciliation, conducted a three-day seminar on 'Connecting Women from Across the LoC' where women from both sides of the border strongly opposed the violence, calling for withdrawal of troops, disbanding of SOG[5] (Special Operations Group) and renegades, as well as the decommissioning of all militant groups operating in Jammu and Kashmir. However, over the years, the impact of the resolution made by the women appears to have had little effect on the peace process politically. Nevertheless, it provided a platform for the women of the two territories to voice their concerns unequivocally.

The center also conducts sensitisation programs for men, mainly college students. Meenakshi Gopinath[6] the founder and incumbent director of WISCOMP has been visiting the colleges regularly and conducting school seminars. Notwithstanding strikes and disturbances in the city, about fifty to sixty percent of the students are able to complete their projects. Women's Studies Centre has a good collection of pencil sketches and portraits of eminent women. A gallery has been created by the reputed artist Muneer Ahmad. In March 2017, the center published a college calendar by the artist, focusing on the women of Kashmir and their professions.

Undeterred by the worsening climate of fear and silence in

---

5 SOG – Special Operations Group is a 1000 – strong elite anti-insurgency force chosen from more than 100,000 troopers of the Jammu and Kashmir Police. It was raised in 1994 with the idea of involving the Jammu and Kashmir Police in anti–terrorist activities and giving a local face to these operations.

---

6 Meenakshi Gopinath is an Indian educationist, political scientist, writer and a former principal of Lady Shri Ram College, New Delhi. She is the founder and incumbent director of the Women in Security Conflict Management and Peace (WISCOMP), a non- governmental organization promoting peace and socio-political leadership among the women of South Asia, and a former member of the National Security Advisory Board, the first woman to serve the Government of India agency.

the last decade, Gurmeet has been able to bring a voice to young students and has thrown open opportunities for dialogue. This program is improving the self-esteem and efficacy of young women, leading them to be critical of their situation and make informed decisions.

Recalling the brutal and inhumane period of the nineties, Gurmeet says that vulnerable and innocent Kashmiri boys were exploited by some leaders who showed them the dream of *azadi* without chalking out and structuring the road to achieve it. The separatist leaders couldn't achieve the expected goals, as their strategy was more about harming others than saving lives.

Prior to 1990, Kashmiris respected and tolerated the differences amongst themselves as they had a legacy of multi-lingual and religious culture. However, Gurmeet is of the opinion that the fundamentalist wave is short-lived and when she sees enthusiastic young boys and girls with a thirst for learning, her hopes for a bright future in the state is strengthened.

Vasanta and Kashyapa Schools—The Educational Legacy that Pandits left behind

Women's Welfare Trust was established in 1926 with the objective of improving the educational and material condition of women. Two schools were opened under the trust—Vasanta Girls High School, Kral Khud, and Kashyapa High School, Chhota Bazar. Gouri Kaul, wife of DN Kaul (First IGP) was the first headmistress of Vasanta School. These schools are the hallmark of women's education in Kashmir that was initiated by the Pandits and gradually spread amongst Muslims as well. These schools should be held as temples of enlightenment for the future generations of women in Kashmir. Today, after 90 years, the schools continue to be shining examples of quality education with modest fees.

Vasanta School

I visited the school in May 2016.The school looked renovated with a fresh coat of paint and I was surprised to find boys and girls playing together in the quadrangle. I talked to the headmistress, Ms Vijay Kaul, who informed me that the trust is headed by the President, Dr GK Mujoo with GL Kaul as the head and secretary of the trust. Mr Shefai and Dr Vimla Dhar are member trustees. Vijay Kaul is the acting headmistress, having taken over from the former headmistress, Shejad Gul. Prior to 1990, the school roll was seven hundred but has come down to three hundred now. Since the roll was low, the school decided to admit boys as well. They charge nominal fees like Kashyapa and run the school on this fee collection. I predictably asked her (as one finds it strange to see a Kashmiri Pandit in Srinagar) the reason for staying in Srinagar. Vijay informed me that her husband who worked for Indian Oil refused to leave the valley in 1990. Her parents and brothers who had already fled to Jammu insisted that she and her family also leave the valley. But they never left.

Earlier, the student ratio was 70% Pandits and 30% Muslims. Now there are no Pandits, but there are some Hindu children from Kishtwar and Doda, Bhaderwah, UP, Bihar and Nepal. Regarding the staff, she says that they have hired new teachers but there is only one Pandit teacher who continues to serve the school like her.

Much of the records and books have been destroyed in the floods of 2014 when the two-storeyed school buildings were under water. Now, one of the buildings has been declared unsafe.

Vasanta School remained closed for only two months during militancy and remained open during the worst of curfews and *hartals* (shutdowns). The school remained open

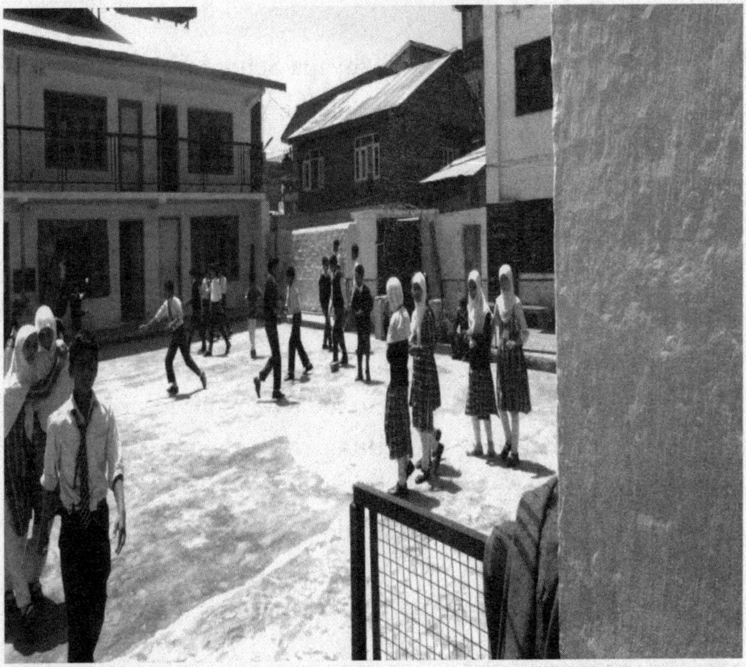

Vasanta School today (2016)

even in 2008, despite the insistence of DIG police to shut the school following the Amarnath yatra imbroglio.

On a personal note, Vijay has had a very good experience with her Muslim colleagues and neighbours. During the floods of 2014 when her house was submerged under water in Karan Nagar, her neighbour offered her shelter in her house and even gave Vijay her own clothes to wear for nearly six months. She feels that even her close relatives would not have done what her Muslim neighbours did for her.

At present, both her sons are living and working in Srinagar and she wants them to get married but no girl is ready to settle in Kashmir. This is posing yet another threat to the miniscule population of Kashmiri Pandits in the valley because the younger generation does not wish to live here.

Kashyapa School

Motilalal Pandita, Principal, Kashyapa School did not migrate after 1990. Dr TN Ganju, one of the trustees of the board, insisted that they should try to salvage the two schools—Vasanta and Kashyapa—and keep them running. Pandita's wife works as a headmistress in a government high school and they have a son and a daughter-in-law who are medical practitioners in Hyderabad.

He informs that most students at present are Muslims and they have only 5-10 Hindu girls in the school. He joined in 1995 and has been managing everything since then as the trustees have given him a free hand. He mentions that about 60-70 government schools have closed down, including schools like Lal Ded High School, DAV, National School, Kamala Nehru School, Vinayak and Arya Putri School. When Motilal Pandita

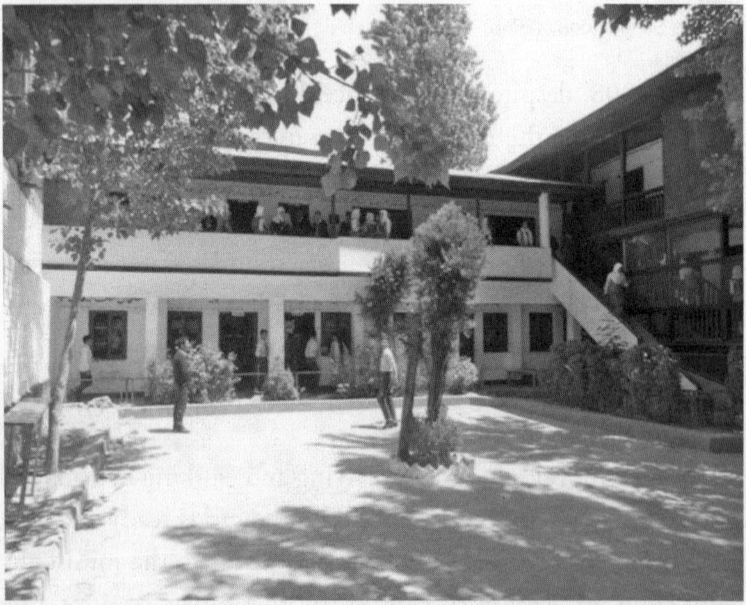

Inside Kashyapa School today (2016)

joined Kashyapa in 1995, it was in ruins. It was burned along with the board bearing the name of the school; water tanks and bathrooms were broken. Undertaking renovation and repair work in the hostile and fearsome environment of the nineties was a challenging task. However, due to the encouragement and support of the trustees, he has not looked back. Pandita says that they have about 400 children on the rolls who come from very poor families and are charged a maximum fee of Rs 500 per month, with a waiver given to orphans. He adds that they have qualified teachers who work on minimum wages and are able to satisfy parental expectations. The only form of revenue is the school fees. There are currently seventeen teachers on the rolls. He says that the widespread unemployment in the valley has forced teachers to work for a paltry salary of Rs 7,000-8,000 per month. Teachers in other schools are not paid during the winter vacation due to inadequate funds. However, since Kashyapa School continues to pay salaries uninterruptedly and provides a congenial environment for the teachers, they are able to retain them. Pandita has been working in the school for the past twenty-one years with a missionary zeal and he says that he is extremely attached to the school and works even on Sundays and holidays.

He remarks that during militancy, there were 10,000 Kashmiri Pandits, but over the years the population has dwindled to a mere 2000-3000. He says that they have no future in Kashmir because the younger generation is not ready to stay in the valley. He gives the example of his son and daughter-in-law, both medical practitioners who are not ready to settle in Kashmir even when they have been born and brought up here. The falling standards of medical practice in both government and private hospitals is very discouraging for them. He says that today doctors are only minting money and providing substandard services, thus forcing common people to seek treatment in cities like Delhi and Mumbai. Though he is often lonely due to his scattered family, Pandita says he will work and continue to live in the valley till his health permits. With the unrelenting support of the trustees, Kashyapa School and Vasanta School will continue to provide quality education to the underprivileged and the poor.

SSM College, Parihaspura, Baramulla

Started in 1998 by Dilafrose Qazi and her husband Dr Shabbir Qazi, the sprawling campus of SSM Institute houses an engineering college, a business management institute, a BEd and a polytechnic college. It is situated near the temple ruins of Parihaspura, the ancient capital of Srinagar during King Laltaditya's reign in the sixth century AD.

SSM College of Engineering is affiliated to the University of Kashmir and approved by the All India Council of Technical Education (AICTE). It has accreditation from National Board of Accreditation. The criterion for admission is based on CET J&K and today there are more than 6,500 students coming from all over the valley. The institute has fifty buses ferrying students and two hostels on the campus. Many students stay in the villages where locals offer their houses on rent. Majority of the students from the civil engineering department are absorbed in the state. They also have campus interviews from BSNL and Reliance and Dilafrose is proud that their alumni are doing exceedingly well all over the world.

What makes SSM special is not its campus but its emphasis on holistic development of the students. One realises Dilafrose's sensitivity to the problems of the youth when she observes that

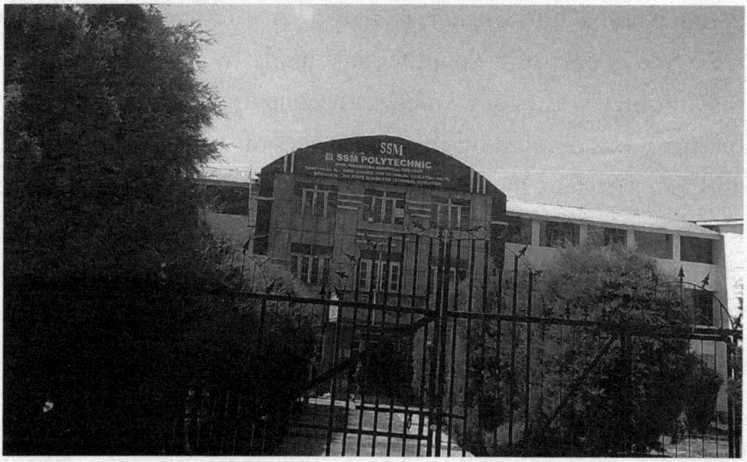

Polytechnic College SSM (2017)

no one smiles anymore in Kashmir. She emphasises that she does not want to just produce professionals; she wants to get the smiles back and make them good human beings. These youngsters have grown up amidst grenade attacks, firing, *hartals* and curfews. There is uncertainty and apprehension all around and most of the students suffer from an identity crisis. She attempts to bring colour to their life by involving them in joyful activities and motivates them to love their life; her constant endeavour has been to deconstruct the root of hatred and negativity.

Apart from running an institute of this size, Dilafrose helps the local community (Shias) residing around the college who work as daily labourers but due to *hartals*, they often have no work and no earnings. She has provided employment to many locals in the college and also arranges general medical camps and maternal and reproductive health camps for women. She also runs technical centers for teaching handicrafts to women.

Many documentaries have been made on Dilafrose's work. As part of their internship, some students from the United

States made a film on her as a woman working in a conflict area. She is part of a documentary made by Doordarshan on inspirational stories of women entrepreneurs. During 1996-98, her story was covered on the front pages of *TOI*, *Indian Express* and *The Hindu*. On a parting note, Dilafrose says,"If we want peace in the valley, we need good educational institutions. When I see my students grow into well-rounded and peace-loving human beings, I am emboldened to change my valley into a true paradise."

Suraiya Ali

A Daughter Fulfills her Mother's Dream

Suraiya Ali, born in Lahore in the early forties, was the youngest of five children born to Sheikh Abdullah and Begum Akbar Jehan. Her maternal grandfather, Ahmed Nedou, the eldest son of the European owner of an Indian hotel chain (that included Nedou's Hotel in Srinagar and Gulmarg) hailed from Austria and converted to Islam after he got married to Suraiya's maternal grandmother Mirjan—a *pahari* girl from Tangmarg. Her parents had seven children, out of which three sons and two daughters survived. Her elder sister Khalida is the wife of Gulshah, erstwhile Chief Minister of J&K; Dr Farooq Abdullah is the second child who also served as Chief Minister of J&K in the eighties; Tariq died almost seven years ago and Dr Mustafa is the secretary of the National Conference, the political party started by Sheikh Mohammad Abdullah, Suraiya's father and a great leader of the state. Their family used to reside in Soura.

Suraiya's elder sister Khalida got married when she was only thirteen years old. However, both the sisters were sent to Mission School (started by Christian missionaries), Fateh Kadal for their early education. Suraiya later went to Maisuma

School, and then shifted to Kothi Bagh School, situated in the premises of Women's College at M A Road. She finished her Masters in English from Kashmir University and served in the Women's College at Maulana Azad Road. In 1971, she married Dr MA Mattoo, a doctor, and their daughter Nyla was born in 1972. Nyla Ali Khan is an eminent writer, presently working at Norman University, Oklahoma. She has written a lot about Kashmir and the political strife with a gender perspective. Some of her famous works include *The Life of a Kashmiri Woman: Dialectic of Resistance and Accommodation, Fiction of Nationality in an Era of Transnationalism, Islam, Women, and Violence in Kashmir: Between India and Pakistan,* and *Sheikh Mohammad Abdullah's Reflections on Kashmir.*

Suraiya retired as a professor of Literature from Women's College in 1999. Talking about the history of education, she says that when the missionaries came to spread western

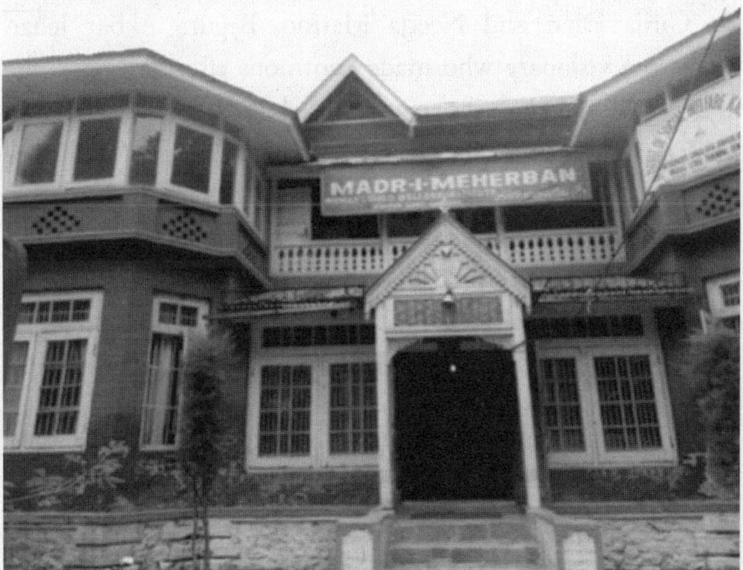

Madr-i-Meherban Welfare Centre, Miskeen Bagh

education in the state in the late nineteenth and early twentieth century, Pandits were the first to sign up, followed by Shias. In an era where maulivis and imams ruled, Miss Mallinson, the first woman missionary faced opposition of unimaginable proportions but she remained undeterred, visited homes and implored parents to send their daughters to school. There were few takers at the time. One person who changed the future of women in Srinagar was Suraiya's mother, Begum Akbar Jehan. She was the first Muslim woman to give up purdah and set a precedent for future generations.

She became the embodiment of modernism by striking the right balance between professionalism and family. Her dream of seeing Kashmiri women, especially Muslim women liberated produced a slew of steely and vibrant women like Begum Zaffar Ali and Begum Jallaludin, Mehmuda Ali, Sajida Zameer (Mehmuda's sister-in-law), Shamla Mufti, Sugra Hafiz, Dr Girija Dhar and Neerja Mattoo. Begum Akbar Jehan was also a visionary who made enormous efforts to serve the underprivileged and the marginalised. In 1974, she started Madr-i-Meherban Welfare Centre for women and children in Miskeen Bagh, Srinagar, and in Gulab Bagh near Ganderbal which housed one hostel for Gujjar and Bakarwal girls (an extremely backward tribe), an orphanage for boys, a craft center, a working women's hostel and a binding and printing press.

By coming to the cities, the Gujjar and Bakarwal girls could get education and also learn various Kashmiri arts and crafts to acquire some skills in order to be economically independent after going back to their villages. Begum Akbar Jehan also started a craft center and a hostel without charging any fees since the center received donations in cash, clothes and kind, which could take care of the running expenses. To fulfill the nutritional needs of this impoverished community, she started a nutrition center where *dals* were sent to various villages to feed mothers and children. Opening a production center where they procured and involved the girls in polishing *dals* indicates her innovative approach to self-reliance, thus enabling many more girls and needy women to earn. As the Gujjar and Bakarwal and also Kashmiri girls started getting jobs in Srinagar, they needed a place to stay. Initially, she arranged a paying guest accommodation for them but soon reports about the girls getting exploited in such an arrangement started pouring in. This prompted her to start a working women's hostel in Miskeen Bagh.

Seeing the mood of the times when destruction and terror ruled in the nineties, Begum Akbar Jehan requested the then Governor to operate the center under the Social Welfare Department. However, after the situation started normalising, the center was handed back to Begum Akbar Jehan. Fortunately, the centers were safe during militancy.

Following the demise of her mother in 2000, Suraiya was asked by her brother, Dr Farooq Abdullah, the then Chief Minister to join the State Social Welfare Board but she did not want to get into the government system. Her sole objective was to run the Madr-i-Meherban Welfare Centre and fulfill her mother's dream of educating the backward and excluded community of Gujjar and Bakarwal girls. Suraiya says that today the center is running on the same lines as it was earlier, but some crafts like carpet-weaving have become defunct and so has *tilla* (silver and gold thread embroidery) work. Now they give training in different kinds of embroidery like crewel, staple work, needle work (*sozini*), cutting and tailoring. They have kept the training center for the printing press and binding books functional. Today, the hostels as well as books and food are government aided. The center also rents out their premises for training *anganwadi* teachers organised through the Social Welfare Department and a building for the Government Girls School where the majority of students belong to Madr-i-Meherban hostel.

Suraiya further says that the upheaval after 1990 changed everything that her family stood for. Secular and liberal voices have been muffled and anarchy and fundamentalist forces have been calling the shots. Pakistan, Iran, and Saudi Arabia are creating an Islamic revolution through the spread of *wahabi* ideology. Pre-1990, they had just one mosque in their neighbourhood, but now she says there are dozens and each one has *azaan* at different times. The *maulvis* give vociferous sermons on the pulpit and this extreme religiosity is impacting everyone, especially women who are persuaded to wear the *hijab*. The separatists want to erase history and downgrade the contribution made by her father Sheikh Abdullah, who spent his entire life fighting for the uplift of Kashmiri people and their rights. Fearing hostility from the separatists, many bookshops are reluctant to stock books written about her father. They call her a traitor's daughter because her father had acceded to India. Suraiya herself has felt threatened many a times and admits that she has restricted her mobility and visits the shops only when required.

She says that they are living in a culture of fear, giving rise to a palpable uneasiness and concealed distrust but she is fortunate to have some like-minded friends.She goes on to say, "How can one restore the trust? Pandits want a guarantee about their safety and security in Kashmir, but when Muslims are not secure, how can security be guaranteed to Pandits? Muslim children who stay out of the valley or abroad wonder why they should return to this *shikas* (wretched place)? In the absence of cinema halls or other entertainment, TV is the only saviour. There is so much *ghutan* (suffocation) here."

Speaking about the youth, Suraiya remarks that children from villages and backward families are getting educated at a huge cost. Families are selling off their paddy land and buying bungalows and big cars, resulting in diminishing rice crop. Schools started by Goenka charge astronomical fees and Delhi Public School is flooded with children from far off districts like Anantnag and Baramulla. Many parents are sending their children out of the state to pursue higher education. Now Kashmiri weddings are being held in Dubai.

Suraiya observes that today there are fewer guns but the separatists come out to face the soldiers and the locals help them to escape. She gives a recent example of Pampore where the Entrepreneur Development Institute building was destroyed by separatists and the fight between the terrorists, police and army continued for three-four days with the support of local people. She says that loyalties are divided and so nobody can be trusted. According to her, this is just lava bubbling on the surface; there are more disturbances on the cards in the future.

She has also observed increasing frustration and aggression amongst youth, which is manifested in them breaking rules and speeding on motorcycles. Youngsters are procuring masters and PhD degrees, but there is no employment. The government has started skill development programs so some do start small businesses but the ones who don't succeed get attracted towards militancy as there is a lot of money being offered to them. Poor and vulnerable youth are lured by money and are told '*Islam ke liye lado*' (fight for Islam). They get swayed by the separatists. The youth in general have become unruly and drug addiction is rampant in the valley.

While talking about the bygone era, one observes a degree of discomfort and forlornness in Suraiya's otherwise calm and dignified demeanor. She recalls the period when she had Pandit and Sikh friends. Their houses were always vibrant and active. It was an era where multiculturalism enriched the cultural, educational and intellectual climate and nurtured artists like Bansi Parimoo and musicians like Shamboo Nath Sopori and his son Bhajan who taught music to Kashmiri boys and girls. Seminars were held for great international and national writers, academicians and scientists. Remarking wistfully, Suraiya says that she would like to revive that culture and hastens to add that Pandits who were prospering in Kashmir have aged prematurely in the hot plains of India. However, there are people who are picking up the shattered pieces of ruination like Dr Girja Dhar, who is keenly involved in ushering the pluralistic climate that has been totally eclipsed now. She has been running an NGO for all these years despite her poor health. Another example is that of Nighat Shafi, who is a diabetic but works tirelessly in conflict-ridden Kupwara.

Although hailing from a powerful political family, Suraiya prefers to keep a low profile and stays detached from forces that are inimical to the pluralistic culture in Kashmir. She declares "we are human beings first" and that is what her family has always valued.

Nighat Shafi

Rebuilding, Reconciling and Healing since the Past Twenty Years

Nighat Shafi was born in 1951 in Srinagar to a family of landlords. Her father, Ghulam Nabi Drabu was the first Muslim postgraduate who studied law in Lahore in the 1920s and '30s.

He was a member of the Public Service Commission. Her mother studied only till 8th standard, but always wanted her daughters to be educated. Nighat says that in those days girls from good families were encouraged to study. Even though her mother did not complete her schooling, her aunts went to college and graduated in 1958-59. However, her grandfather was very keen that they stay grounded and encouraged them to do all the household chores. Nighat did her schooling from Presentation Convent, Rajbagh, and completed her Bachelors in Economics, English literature and Education from Women's College, Srinagar. She got married in 1970 to Mohammed Shafi Pandit who served in the Indian Administrative Service in various capacities. She followed her husband and his work, and lived in the capital for fifteen years over two tenures. Nighat has three children—a son and two daughters who are all settled abroad. She and her husband have been based in Srinagar since 1997.

Recalling the period of militancy, she says that the dark period witnessed a lot of bloodshed and pain; human life was lost on all sides. In 1995, her husband, who was then the Additional Chief Secretary in Srinagar, had a narrow escape. About 30-odd militants attacked him when he was visiting his sister's place. The police and the army were summoned, cross firing lasted for 3-4 hours and two civilians were also killed. However, this incident did not deter Nighat and her husband from extending help in the strife-torn state. Shafi advised her to start her own NGO and get it registered so that she could gain credibility. That marked the birth of Human Effort for Love and Peace (HELP Foundation) in J&K in 1997, which was started with the primary objective of organising a social response to the growing destitution and distress resulting from the decades-long turmoil in Jammu and Kashmir State.

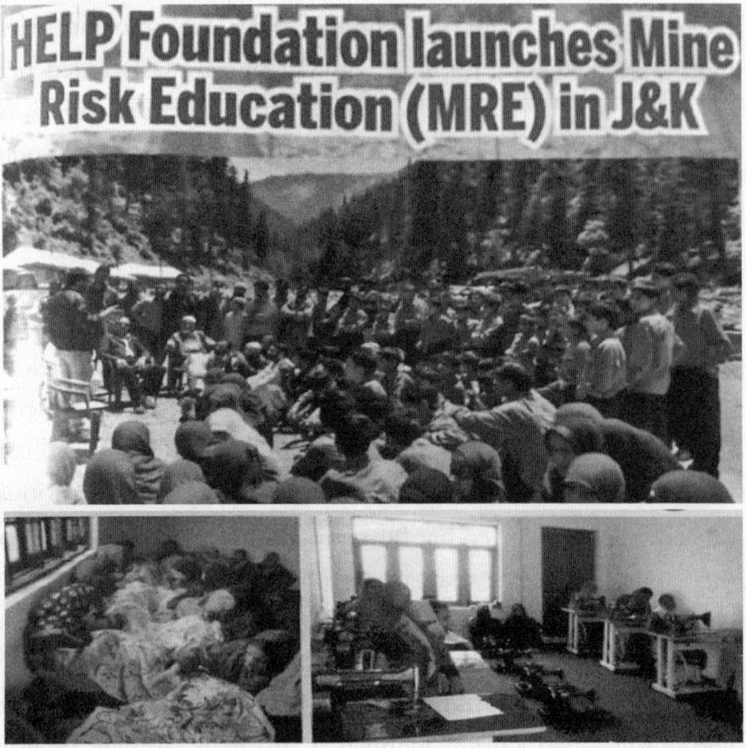

Skill development at Ganderbal

Nighat made her initial efforts in Shanpora, the backwaters of the Dal. When she asked women what they wanted, they said that they really wanted their children to go to school as all the schools around had been burnt down. She started a school in a rented two-room house and within some days, 150 children were enrolled up to the 10th standard. However, this lasted for a short time as schools in the area restarted once restoration and renovation work had been completed. As she interacted with people, she was faced with a deluge of issues. Continual conflict and disturbance had impacted the emotional and mental health of women, children and young adults, leading to depression and drug addiction, especially amongst the youth.

Unemployment and rise in social issues like domestic violence and suicide cases have further exacerbated the dismal situation in the valley since militancy. With grit and determination, she faced them all.

In 1997, Nighat started an orphanage with 30 children that has expanded to 250 today. She runs three schools with a roll of 500-700 children at Inderhama, Srinagar, and Khumrial, Kupwara, where orphans and underprivileged children are not only getting school education (either free of cost or with token fees), but are being sponsored for professional courses as well. She proudly says that these students go on to complete MBAs or become doctors and get employment in Delhi. One boy was sponsored for higher education in England and another girl received a Fullbright scholarship. Aside from this, remedial education and special education facilities have been set up for 'specially abled' children in Srinagar and Kupwara.

As a response to this grave and challenging situation of deteriorating mental health, HELP Foundation initiated work with Kashmir University for this. In fact, it is the first NGO to start a mental health clinic (in operation since 2002) in Karan Nagar along with Aman Trust from Delhi, with the help of Dr Arshad, a leading psychiatrist of Kashmir. Nighat says that there is rampant consumption of *charas*, cough syrup, glue and boot polish; she has even seen 6-year olds addicted to some form of drugs. Counselling centers for de-addiction and special cells for domestic violence, including a helpline for legal aid, have been opened. She reports that they have youth on the waiting list for 3-4 months, who are desperate to seek help but do not want to be hospitalised because of social stigma. They provide a space for the addicts where they can vent their problems and interact freely. They have also witnessed boys being sexually assaulted by *maulvis*

(Muslim priests). These incidents led to the formation of a 24x7 CHILDLINE (Toll-Free #1098) for children in distress, set up under a national program (ICPS) administered by the Ministry of Women & Child Development (MWCD), Government of India, in Hyderpura. This has contributed in spreading a lot of awareness on Child Rights. For suicide prevention, they have been counselling families for the last sixteen years and equipping them with problem solving skills.

The situation of women, especially widows, has been pathetic during the last twenty years. Kupwara, a border district town had been totally devastated during militancy and has the highest number of widows. Nighat runs skill development courses in Kupwara for girls in the morning and boys in the evening. For economic supplementation, the Foundation is providing vocational training in craft, cutting, tailoring, food processing and computer education in Ganderbal, Beeru, Kupwara, Baramulla and Srinagar. They also provide grants and/or interest free loans to needy women to help them initiate or expand their micro-business in the house/community. Women produce spices, snacks, Ari work (chain stitch embroidery) and pashmina and kani shawls which are marketed at Shehjaar (a marketing outlet of the Foundation) in Rajbagh, Srinagar. Micro-financing projects have also been in operation and at present there are 2,500 members in all five districts. The Foundation also operates a clinic for women where free medicines are distributed. The clinic has a mammography machine for breast cancer screening during village camps.

NABARD, Save the Children, Action Aid and Tata Trust are supporting HELP Foundation. Aside from its work in the valley, the Foundation has set up ten schools in Jammu. Not leaving any sector untouched, HELP has been prompt in responding to both natural and man made calamities. During floods, it provided interest-free loans to ten boys and girls who set up entrepreneurship activities like medical shops and student cafés. As part of the project for prevention of injuries and deaths related to mines in border areas of Rajouri, Poonch, Kupwara and Baramulla, HELP collaborated with Handicap International for rehabilitation of mine victims and provided them with prosthetics. Other projects include the Godfrey Philips-supported (as part of their CSR—Corporate Social Responsibility), beautification of Pratap Park which was badly damaged during the floods.

Attempting to uphold the unique, inclusive and secular values of the social, cultural and religious society of Kashmir, the Foundation has used innovative methods for impacting young minds that can influence future generations with their altered mindsets and world view. She explains that when the elite class left the Valley during militancy, there was a lot of infiltration of Muslims from outside who transported the *Barelvi* and *Wahabi* ideology of Islam as opposed to the *Sufi* tradition in the Valley where people had a more emancipated perspective of religion. She says that there is a different Islam being practised beyond Banihal (the entry point into the valley). Nighat further reiterates that a lot of money has been pumped through the *maulvis* and *imams* who are involved in radicalising Islam and expanding their influence.

Against these social and political realities, Nighat redefined education and strategically emphasised peace and brotherhood in her dialogues, whether it was with under-trials or with school children. They have been doing a lot of theatre with children. In 2000, they introduced theatre in the schools to explore the potential and talent in the children, and to lessen their stress levels with a therapeutic outlet. This also helped eliminate the diktat, which forced people to have no entertainment in the region. Children born after the exodus of Kashmiri Pandits in 1990 have seen a homogenous society deprived of multi-cultural vibrancy which was a hallmark of the pre-militancy era. Saddened by this reality, Nighat recreated how Kashmiri Pandits and other ethnic communities in the valley lived exhibiting their dress, culture and different festivals, through theatre and fashion shows. Feisal Alkazi, an educationist, trainer and theatre director from Delhi, did a six-month workshop on Kashmiri heritage which HELP published as a training module prompting the then Governor to recommend it as part of the school curriculum in J&K.

Besides chairing the HELP Foundation, Nighat has been an honorary Member of the Board of Directors of the J&K State Women's Development Corporation since 2010. She is also working in an advisory capacity with reputed organisations at the state and national levels including Ford Foundation, AFPRO (Action for Food Production), J&K State Women's Commission, J&K State Rehabilitation Council, Kashmir Women's Credit Co-operative Ltd, and was offered Board membership for National Commission for Protection of Child Rights. Her determination in facilitating peace building and harmony in conflict areas has been reflected by her engagement with organisations like Centre for Dialogue & Reconciliation, Delhi Policy Group. Additionally, HELP Foundation, in collaboration with an internationally reputed organisation, MANFORD, has been organising workshops with functionaries involved in the process of governance, in order to bring about appropriate behavioural orientation for facilitating the process of sustainable development and peace building in the region.

For her bold initiatives and social activities in the conflict region, Nighat was selected as one of the 1000 women around the globe, nominated jointly for a Nobel Peace Prize under the *1000 Peace Women Project* in 2005. At national level, she has been honoured with numerous awards including *Stree Shakti Award* (Women's Empowerment Award) by the Government of India consecutively for three years from 2005-06 to 2007-08, *Asian Peace Award* and *Mehjoor Award* in 2007 and 2010 respectively and *Jamnalal Bajaj Award* for distinguished social work for the development of women and children in the year 2012.

Although Nighat has kept herself away from politics and religion, she says that it is very difficult to work in Kashmir as people have a lot of vested interests. When she started work, rumours were circulated that she was spreading Christianity. She remarks sadly, "I do not know how long I will last. Whenever I need anything, my team is there. Our trustees are old and younger people see this work through the single lens of *what is in it for me?*" Currently, she has a staff of 250, but she wants to consolidate and cut down on work. Remarking on the exodus of Kashmiri Pandits, she says, "We can all live together but the politicians will not let us do so. Everybody is making quick bucks here. There is no accountability and as an NGO, we cannot get into the political system."

In future, HELP's focus will be on children and youth in Juvenile homes, with under-trials and released prisoners using counselling, theatre workshops and behavioural skills to change their attitudes so that they are better equipped to face society. For Nighat, mental and emotional health of people takes precedence over all interventions as she believes it to be crucial for bringing peace and reconciliation in the valley.

Nazir Benazir: Spotlighting Environment in Times of Conflict

Nazir Benazir was born in 1953 in Nawa Bazar, Srinagar, and passed his graduation from Government College, Bemina with Economics and Political Science as his main subjects. He has three children and has been running a business but the turmoil and terrorism that followed in the years after 1990 have made him helpless. Fearing that environmental issues would get ignored in the climate of terror and destruction, Benazir resolved to follow his dream of saving the environment and formed the National Society for Water resources, Wetlands and Forests (NSWWF) in 1995. This was done on a voluntary basis because he wanted to save the depleting natural resources of the state—be it water bodies, springs, waterfalls, rivers or glaciers. He believes that if these resources are lost, Kashmir will lose its *wajood* (identity) and everything it stood for. Agriculture and horticulture are intricately dependent on these natural resources and if these are degraded, then the state will perish. Thus, NSWWF began its journey by collaborating with the Forest department, school children and youth by spreading awareness in schools and colleges and amongst land owners (Zamindars) and communities.

Strategically, the Society decided to roll out their initial interventions through school children as they are enthusiastic about bringing about changes in their surroundings. The first project was targeted on the usage of polythene and its impact on the environment and agriculture. With the participation of school children, the society took an oath promising to themselves that, "*Hum riyasate Jammu and Kashmir ko jannate Benazir nahin kahenge, jab tak hum polythene ko nahin hatayenge*" (We will not call Kashmir a paradise unless we remove polythene from here). The program was sustained through school children for a couple of months, but adults did not take it seriously. The then Environment Minister declared that he would make Kashmir polythene-free. However, like all public programs, perseverance and follow-up is the key to sustained impact which cannot happen without the involvement of forestry or other concerned departments. Nonetheless, for many years now, polythene is not being used in shops in Srinagar but vegetable vendors still use them.

The next project involved planting saplings on the ancient Shankaracharya temple hill. During the early sixties, the hill was barren and bare. GM Sadiq, the then Chief Minister, made efforts to increase the forest cover but during militancy, the hill started turning barren again. In 1995, again with the help of school children and NSWWF, reforestation of the hill was undertaken and today it is a dense forest once again.

Benazir says that they have worked in far flung areas along the Pir Panjal Range with school children who have planted five lakh saplings with the help of forestry and other departments. Each child sows one plant and goes back to monitor its growth.

NSWWF also started working at a community level, visiting villages and spreading awareness about the linkage between environment and livelihood. For example, a wetland like Hokersar, which is home to three lakh migratory birds from Siberia and Central Asia, has been on the verge of turning into a dumpyard since many years due to encroachments and industrial and household pollutants. It was a thriving ecosystem providing food to the migratory birds and to the inhabitants who live around it. The lake provided lotus stem (nadru), fish, vegetables and water chestnuts and the sale of the produce was a source of income for the villagers since decades. Also, in times of floods, Hokersar used to absorb much of the flood waters, but in 2014, the flood waters could not be contained because of shrinking area and formation of silt, giving rise to a water level that reached two floors or more in low lying areas. Although poaching is legally disallowed, it continues as there are many entries to the wetland. The NSWWF, along with the department of Forestry, has been able to spread awareness in the villages around Hokersar and today the encroachments have significantly reduced.

Benazir paints a very depressing picture of the valley as far as its environment is concerned. He says that with the increasing population, the pattern of land use has changed over the years and impacted the environment. Once Dachigam Nallah used to supply water to the whole city but now people are using water from the Dal Lake for drinking. Sixty percent of springs have disappeared along with Ropa Lank, Sona Lank and Telbal spring waters. There was once a spring called Kohnaraz Nag

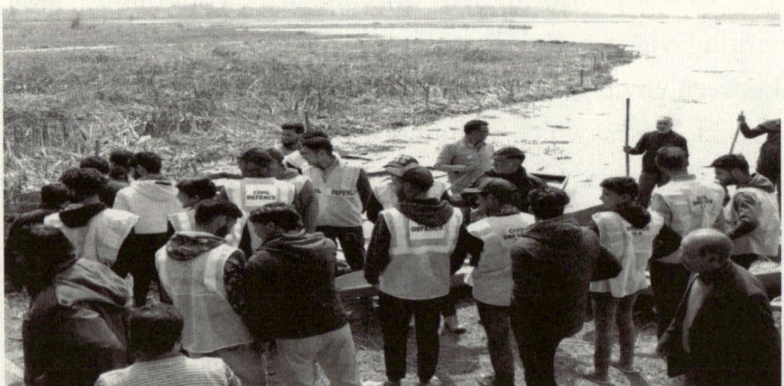

Cleaning Hokersar (2018)

at Sazgaripura Road, Hawal, on the way to Tulla Mulla, an ancient shrine of the Pandits. *Yatris* (travellers) would stay for the night at Kohnaraz Nag and then proceed to Tulla Mulla the next day. Vicharnag spring has also been destroyed. Buildings have come up on top of springs that had cold water in summer and hot water in winters. Benazir further adds that there will be fights for water in the future and dams and rivers will become international properties. He adds in a sarcastic tone, "It will soon be *sasta khoon* aur *mehenga pani* (blood will be cheaper than water)."

Due to lax municipal permissions, agricultural lands have been transformed into concrete residential colonies. As multi-storeyed buildings are legally disallowed, more and more land is being encroached upon for making residential bungalows. Indra Nagar, which used to be a wetland, has been encroached by land-filling and houses were constructed on it about forty years back. More than 14,000 canals of apple orchards have been converted to residential colonies, leading to low yield of apples. Now apples are imported from outside.

Rahi Riaz, who is a member of NSWWF and a close aide of Benazir, says that working without funds many times hinders their passion for this work. At times they do not even have fifty rupees in their pocket to fill petrol but they have been managing somehow. Benazir is on the advisory board as executive committee member or chairperson of many government and non-government organisations like Compensatory Afforestation Fund Management and Planning Authority (CAMPA) under the Ministry of Environment, Forests and Climate Change. After so many years of work, schools now call them on 5th June to celebrate World Environment Day, and every year in March, the schools proudly show their plantations to Society members. Even in an atmosphere of fear and impending terror, the army, CRPF and para-military forces have always supported them. NSWWF conducts educational trips to Dachigam (a sanctuary and an example of biodiversity) with college students and it is wonderful to see youth taking a deep interest in how the environment is intricately linked to human survival. Benazir remarks, "One cannot get educated in classrooms, children have to move out, be it curfew or *hartal*." Benazir has won many laurels—the Jammu University Award, Kashmir University Award, etc. What started as voluntary work has become his mission. He remarks cheerlessly that the government allocation for environment is only 0.4% of its annual budget but the society continues to work in collaboration with the department of Forestry and is inadvertently ensuring that the budget gets utilised. He has travelled extensively in the state to see the forests of Ladakh and Zanskar. The organisations that he is associated with support his travel and accommodation, but he is not financially compensated for his services. Over the years, his enthusiasm hasn't diminished because of his meagre earnings and he hastens to add that he prefers to continue this work without any monetary involvement because he believes that money can corrupt.

He feels that the militancy in 1990 was a political issue and should be dealt with politically. Geographically and culturally, there is no difference between India and Pakistan, and for both the countries, unless there is peace, there will be no development.

Benazir says that the impact on the environment affects neighbouring countries too—if Jhelum gets flooded, then both India and Pakistan will suffer—perhaps alluding to the social environment too that permeates across borders. He proudly declares that Kashmir is an example of secularism, famous for hosting guests (*mehman nawazi*) and has always believed in humanism.

Rahi Riyaz Ahmed

The Lone Crusader Who Expanded His Tribe

Rahi Riyaz Ahmed was born on 26 September 1976 in Gund Hassi Bhat, Srinagar. He is married with four children. He is a postgraduate in Arts. At the onset of militancy and political disturbances in 1989, he was a teenager studying in Class 9, when he witnessed widespread destruction and a reign of terror and disaster. Rahi says that everything was impacted—educational institutions, forests, health services. All sectors became victims of militancy and political apathy. He says passionately, "I wanted to do something, something to save the future of my land, something to bring the education sector back on track, something to preserve the green gold and something that could make a difference... I wanted to save my paradise from becoming a hell. This passion of doing my bit to protect and preserve Kashmir resulted in the formation of AHSAN Foundation J&K on 1 January 1998." His area of operation is confined to eight districts with focused work in Budgam, Pulwama and some parts of Srinagar.

Rahi's strength is his resourcefulness in creating a band of earnest volunteers who get trained in health (including blood donation, immunisation, holding medical camps and increasing accountability of public health services), education, environment conservation and networking with various public and private social service organisations. He works closely with the departments of Health, Education, Social Forestry, Wildlife, Forest Department, Srinagar Municipal Corporation and Department of Civil Defence. He also works with Central

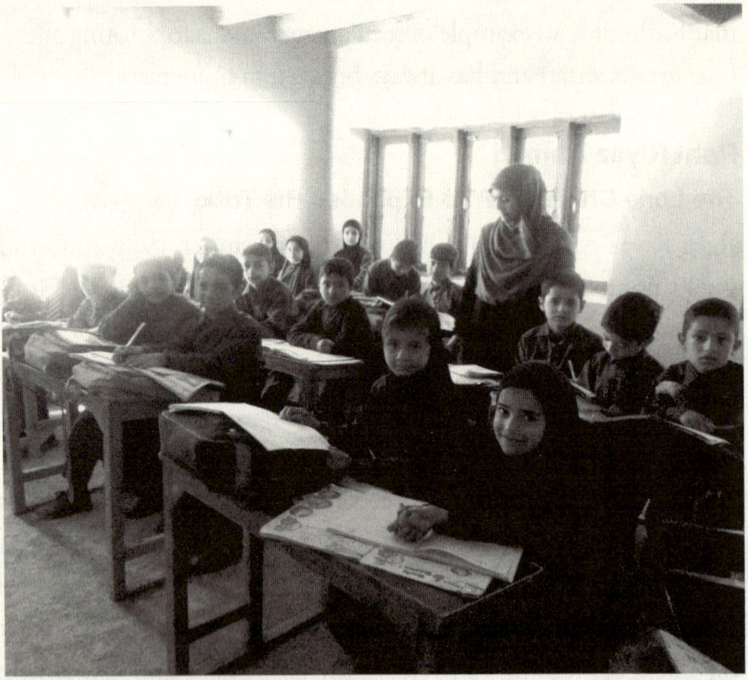

Rahi Public School, Lawaypora (2016)

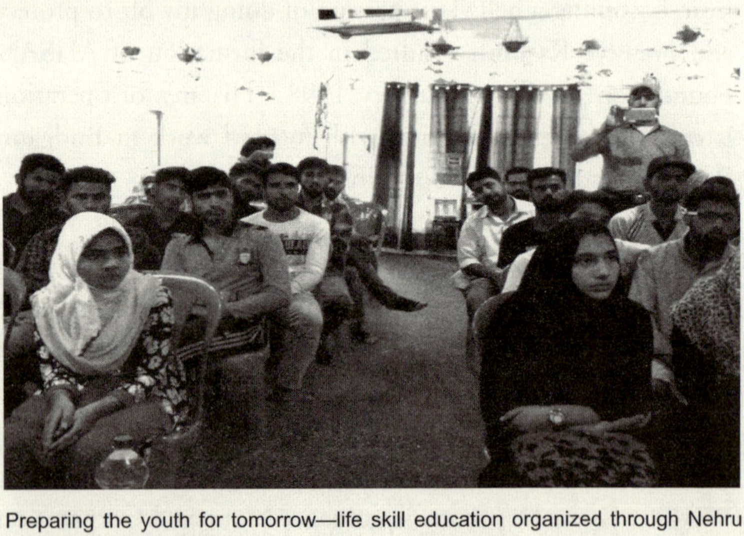

Preparing the youth for tomorrow—life skill education organized through Nehru Yuva Kendra (July 2018)

boards for workers' education through Ministry of Labour and Employment, Govt of India.

During the period of militancy (1991-95), health services were impacted the most aside from education. Rahi says that there were maximum numbers of maternal deaths because women (particularly from remote villages) could not reach the hospital due to shutdowns. This prompted him to think innovatively. With the health department's help, he trained educated girls and Anganwadi workers in the villages to deal with maternal health emergencies particularly for pregnant women and those in labour. Since then, he has been making health services available to people by conducting medical camps in collaboration with government and private doctors.

Apart from providing free/subsidised medicines to needy patients through pharmaceutical companies, AHSAN has also been involved in conducting immunisation and pulse polio camps in collaboration with the health department. The organisation also conducts house to house survey for TB control and refers patients to PHCs (Primary Health Centres) and CHCs (Community Health Centres). AHSAN volunteers in collaboration with the Department of Civil Defence, have participated in several training programmes on First Aid, CPR (Cardio Pulmonary Resuscitation) and Disaster Management. Rahi has also attended a training program on Disaster Management conducted by AWO International e.V. Germany in 2007.

Another critical contribution by AHSAN is making blood available to needy patients. Once he saw a man abandoning his wife who needed blood because he did not have the means to do so. Finally, her father-in-law was ready to give blood and she was saved. Incidents like this led him to spread awareness about blood donation through camps. Since the past many years, he has motivated a band of 1500 volunteers who donate blood and are available on call. The patients call the blood bank directly which in turn call the volunteers to donate blood.

Rahi has also arranged blood donations camps in collaboration with J&K Voluntary Health and Development Association. He, a role model himself, has donated blood many times along with his volunteer, Shabir Khan. The blood is stored in the government blood banks and they regularly donate in Lal Ded, SMHS and Barzulla Bone and Joint Hospital. They encourage patient's relatives to donate one bottle in exchange of one from the blood bank. However, if there are no relatives, then blood is provided without any donation in return. Rahi also arranges health camps for schools and colleges where medical checkups and blood donation drives are conducted.

AHSAN has also been instrumental in getting the pending incentives of Anganwadi and ASHA workers released from the health department. He has conducted two workshops through an advocacy group called Common Health (a coalition for neonatal and maternal health and safe abortion services) on Training and Accountability for Maternal Health. As a fallout of this, AHSAN volunteers are using checklists of the services that should be available in a public health facility.

In 1992 when schools were shut down, Rahi motivated civil society *mohalla* committee members to start tuition classes for children in Budgam, Bandipore and Srinagar districts. Similarly, during the floods of 2014 when schools were closed, his volunteers swung into action to teach children. He is proud that his volunteers never hesitate to respond to social and environment disasters. He also distributes school uniforms, notebooks and text books for poor students through his consortium of NGOs.

Since educational institutes were the first casualty of militancy, Rahi started Rahi Public School in 1995 for a mixed population of BPL(Below Poverty Line) and orphaned children. He proudly claims that his alumni have become engineers and doctors. In wake of the closure of schools during political strife, he has guided many of his students to open schools throughout the valley. His main source of revenue is fee collection but since many of the children are poor, their fees are waived.

Rahi is also the General Secretary of National Society for Water resources, Wetlands and Forests (NSWWF) since 1995 and has collaborated with the Office of the Wildlife Warden, Wetlands, Kashmir for conservation of wildlife, particularly wetlands in Hokersar. His involvement has provided him opportunities to participate in symposiums related to the impact of climate change on migratory birds. Since 2001, he has been arranging awareness programmes like essays, debates, painting competitions and is involved in eco development programmes to uplift the downtrodden and destitute community living on the fringes of wetlands. Through the Central Board for Workers Education, Ministry of Labour and Employment, GOI, he has received training in various types of government and social security schemes for rural and unorganised workers. Zealous in transferring his knowledge to people, he says that he is a bridge between the common public and government and makes people aware about different government schemes and facilities. He has guided many women to open self-help groups. Till date, about 100 self-help groups have been started in the state.

He has earned many laurels like medals from Director General of Civil Defence, New Delhi, and other government departments for his meritorious service. He has also received the

Tata Virtual National Fellowship (2007) for Rural Prosperity.

Braving innumerable hardships during the years of political turmoil and militancy, Rahi continues to be an inspiration for a large number of youth volunteers who see him as a role model and continue to serve the society in times of conflict and disasters.

Hasrat Gadda

The Last Scion of Symbiotic Art, Culture and Language in Kashmir

GR Hasrat Gadda was born in 1937 in downtown Srinagar and was the only child of his parents. He passed his matriculation from Government State School, Baghe Dilawer Khan (later renamed MP High School), Fateh Kadal, famous for producing personalities like Prem Nath Bazaz, Dinanath Nadim and Sheikh Mohammad Abdullah. His father was a Gandhian and was even jailed for his participation in the freedom struggle in 1945. Hasrat has three children, two sons and a daughter who all live in Srinagar. He started working in 1958 and due to his literary leanings, he became a member of Halqa Alima Adab in Khanyar—a literary and cultural organisation managed by late Gulam Mohammad Sadiq that had illustrious members like Rahman Rahi, Dinanath Nadim, Pushkar Nath, Avtar Krishen Rahbir and Ghulam Nabi Firaq. In 1962, he started writing poetry, which was published in two newspapers of Hamdard—*Khadmat* and *Martand*. He later joined the J&K Cultural Academy as literary and cultural activities in-charge and got trained at Lalit Kala Academy, Delhi, for display and exhibition of paintings. He was subsequently appointed as an exhibition officer at the J&K Cultural Academy and formally retired in 1995. Gadda is a member of a dozen literary organisations like

Kashmiri Cultural Organisation, Koshur Markuz, Funkaar Cultural Organisation and others.

Recalling the year of 1990, he says that on 29 January of that year, he was operated upon at SKIMS hospital in Soura and had twenty-five stiches. But as soon as his friend, Retinder Kaul came to see him, Gadda was immediately asked to leave the hospital by the authorities as they feared that he and his Pandit friend were informers. They fled immediately. Four years later, Gadda was kidnapped but released immediately after the abductors realised that they would not be able to extort any money from a writer. Undeterred by personal and other mass incidents of extortion and destruction, shut downs, crackdowns and cross firing, Gadda arranged cultural activities, painting competitions and exhibitions during militancy. He formed Funkaar Cultural Organisation that held exhibitions on the Rishi cult in Government College of Education in 1994. He has also written innumerable books on the cultural and linguistic heritage of Kashmir. He has translated works of poets like Dinanath Nadim, Abdul Qadir Dervish and a compilation on Master Zinda Kaul is underway. He is an expert on Kashmiri music, literature and painting and boasts of a personal library with over 10,000 books.

He has received many laurels that include an award from Athwas Foundation, Jammu, for meritorious service in the field of theatre, Radio and TV by Bakshi Mermind Committee (named after former Prime Minister Jenab Bakshi Mohammad); Award of Honour, Jammu University, Jammu; Sadiq Mohammad Committee Award for Culture (named after former Chief Minister GM Sadiq); Gulshan Books Award for Culture and Literature; March for Peace Award given by Lt General SK Sinha, Governor J&K State; Rabindra Nath

Tagore Award by the Gandhi family for contribution in the field of Literature and Cultural Studies; award by Department of Urdu, Jammu University and RJMLS Society, Jammu; Gandhi Memorial Award given by former Chief Minister, Ghulam Nabi Azad.

In 2008, he brought out a magazine called *Kashmir Insight,* featuring the unique linguistic and cultural heritage of the state. He publishes this magazine on a no profit basis. Gadda appears to be a lone crusader, finding it difficult to publish his magazine with his diminishing funds. He says that he has influenced a lot of people with his secular views and created a pool of fifty to sixty like-minded people like writer and educationist MH Zafar; poet, writer and literary critics like Shabir Ahmed Shabir, Rehman Rahi (poet) and many others. He draws a parallel between different historical situations; earlier people died because of famine, small pox and cholera, now the gun or *bandook* culture has wiped out people along with their cultural roots. Still, substantial work on Kashmiri literature and culture was produced in the mid-nineties but unfortunately many of those writers are not living.

He has written articles on Kashmir Shaivism and works by Pandit poets like Permanand, Bulbul Nagami, Master Zinda Kaul and Dinanath Nadim who wrote on social justice. He has tried to save the unique symbiotic Kashmiri culture from the tsunami of terrorism and fundamentalist ideologies in the worst of times. He adds that Kashmir valley has forty archaeological sites and Jammu has ten, but the Archeological Survey of India office has been shifted to Jammu, pointing to the declining interest by the state administration in saving these sites. He also says that many temples are in a terrible condition but nobody cares. There is no art gallery in Kashmir whereas there are four in Jammu. There are five district cultural centres of art, culture and language in Jammu (Doda, Kashtwar, Bhaderwah, Kathua, and Rajouri) but there is no such cultural centre existing in Kashmir valley. Even Ladakh and Kargil both have cultural centres. He appears helpless and regretful seeing the rich multicultural fabric of the valley on its last legs.

Talking about *azadi* in Kashmir, he says that Kashmiri people do not want to be a part of Pakistan. Pakistan is in

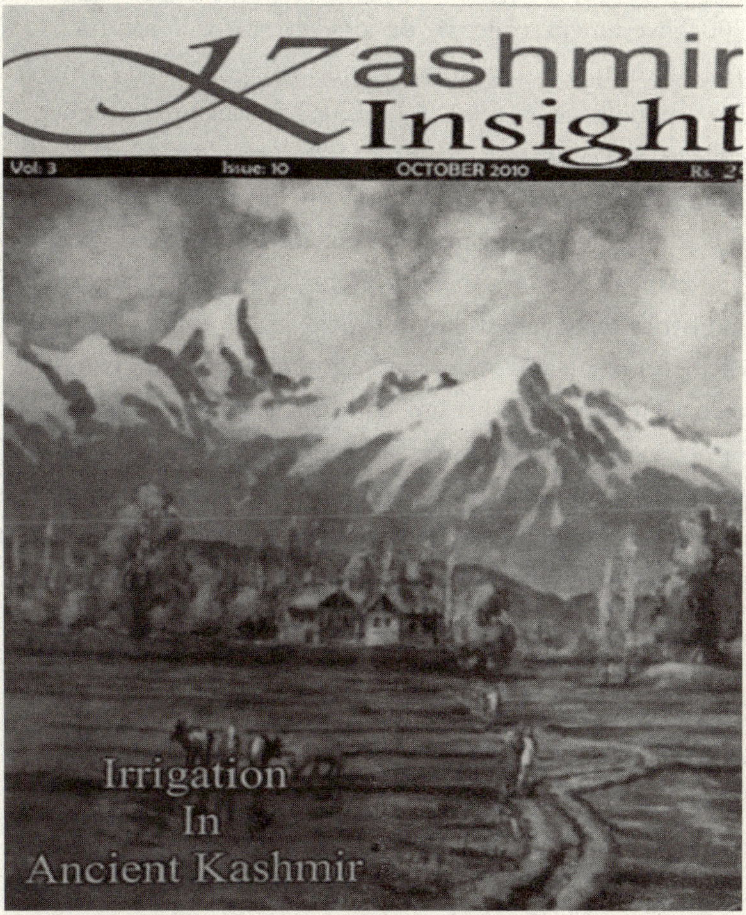

A sample of Gadda's publication

shambles and so is Pakistan controlled Kashmir. He had visited POK (Pakistan Occupied Kashmir) some years ago and found that the place was underdeveloped, with low literacy rate and only one university. In comparison, Kashmir valley has four universities: Agricultural University, Kashmir University, Central University, and Islamic University. There are four medical colleges, one each in Baramulla and Anantnag and two in Srinagar. There is an NIT (National Institute of Technology) and many private engineering colleges, 10 nursing colleges and 200 government colleges. Besides, every *tehsil* has one ITI and more than 5,000 primary and higher secondary schools. For a population of 69,07,622, (2011 census), the number of colleges and educational institutes are disproportionately huge.

Yet there is large-scale unemployment. Gadda believes that this is due to faulty planning; there are 5,000 skilled youth or professionals being trained for every 1,000 jobs. There are no industries or organisations instituted in the valley to support them. Rampant corruption in the government sector is another menace where one either has to grease the palms of the officials or get a *sifarish (*recommendation). Government of India has pumped in thousands of crores for Dal development and power development. So many tunnels are under construction but there is no accountability. He says regretfully, *"Common people here are not mad, they have been led to madness."*

Perceiving himself to be the last scion, he says indefatigably that as long as he breathes, he will not give up declaring proudly, *"My culture is as much Hazratbal (a revered Muslim shrine) or Nund Rishi (Muslim saint) as it is Tulla Mulla (most revered Hindu temple of Ragynadevi) or Lal Ded (Hindu saint). My culture is a composite linkage of Hindu Muslim Unity in Kashmir."*

Sajad Ahmed

Channelising Youth towards Sports

Sajad Ahmed was born in 1970 in Magam, district Budgam, Kashmir. He did his schooling from Government Middle School, Magam, and completed his higher secondary from Boys Higher Secondary School in the same town. After 12th standard, he completed his diploma and bachelor's degree in martial arts from Hanuman Vyayam Nagar, Amravati, Maharashtra. Although, Sajad is employed as a teacher in the local Middle School for girls, it is his childhood passion for sports and martial arts that is keeping him rooted to his birth place. He introduced walking/jogging and exercise amongst his peers and influenced the diabetic and overweight to exercise thus becoming a role model for the youth in his town. In 2010, he opened a sports club called Spartan Martial Club in the same town, teaching martial arts like Taekwondo, Wusho and Karate. Through his club, he trains children to participate in state and national level championships.

Owing to his warm and inspiring personality, he is gradually influencing mothers to send their daughters to the club. Till date, 200 girls have passed out from his club—a rare feat in Kashmir. In 2017, his club won one brass and one gold medal in Taekwondo in the School National Games held at national level. Sajad says that he only charges rupees hundred as membership fees but does not charge separately for coaching. Till date, about 500 children have been trained in his club. Apart from running the club, he contributes to social causes also. He volunteers to clean rivers, streams and ponds in his town along with other volunteers. By continuing to provide such opportunities to small town girls and boys, Sajad has created history in times of conflict and despair.

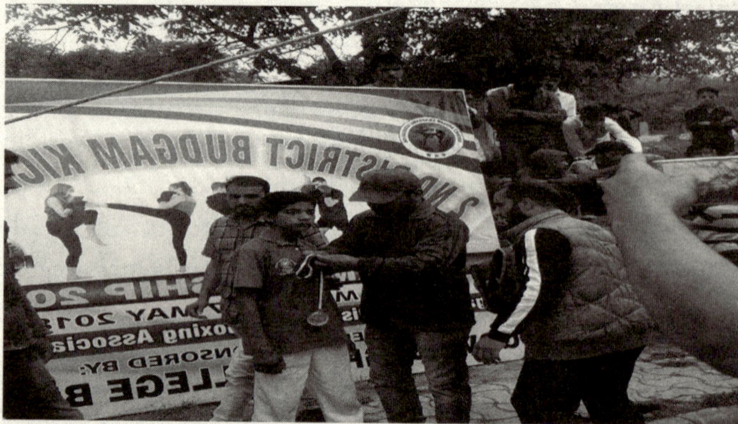

Sajad (in blue jacket) conferring a medal to the winner for Kick Boxing (2018)

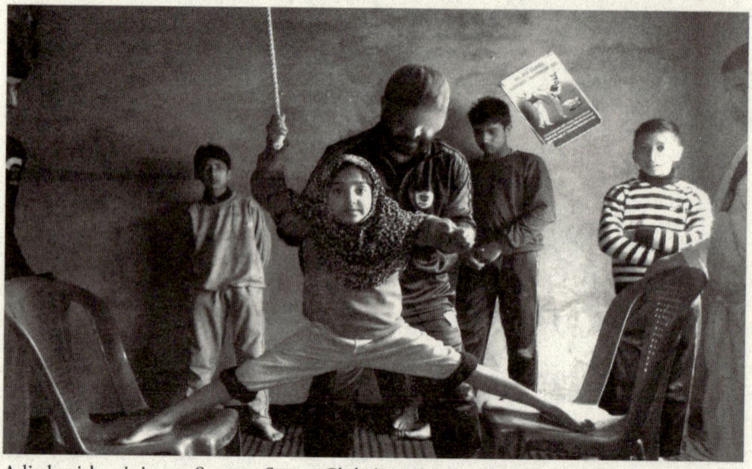

A little girl training at Spartan Sports Club (2018)

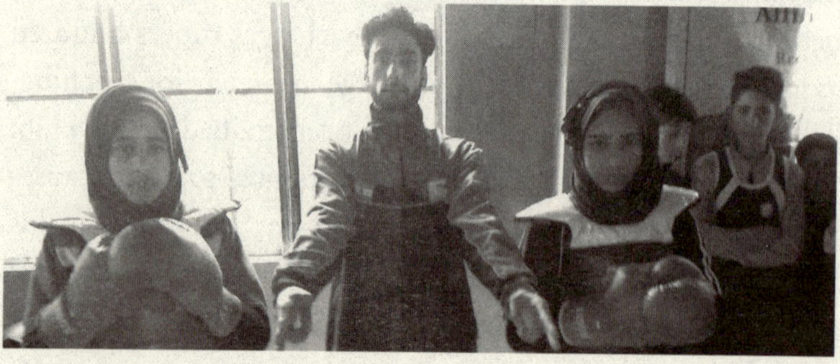

Girls Kick Boxing (2018)

Other Initiatives

NGOs like Guild for Services (GFS), a national voluntary development organisation is working with women and children. They started Rahat Ghar, a shelter home for conflict affected children and women under the Government of India's Swadhar scheme in the valley. Guild For Services also has shelter homes in Vrindavan, Godhra and Sawai Madhopur and various other projects that nourish, support and empower women. In earlier years, Rahat Ghar provided admission to both boys and girls, but now, the organisation has decided to focus on the girl child. Supported by the Department of Women and Child Development, the home provides children material comforts as well as the opportunity for self-development. The shelter home was started in 2000 at Kupwara and later was shifted to Zakura. At present, it is housed in Chandilora, Tangmarg and 65 girls are admitted in the shelter home. These girls go to local schools during the day and attend tuitions for Maths and religious teachings in the evening.

Besides these activities, they are involved in sports like cricket and volleyball as well as in gardening. The older girls look after the younger ones. Many of them are excellent singers and have performed at local and national level programmes arranged through Guild For Services. Most of the mothers are either widowed or separated or those whose husbands have disappeared. The mothers visit Rahat Ghar regularly and the girls in turn visit their homes during Eid and winter vacations. The woman behind this endeavour is the director, Jaya Iyer. She has been looking after the shelter home since the past eighteen years under the guidance of Dr Girija Dhar, Chairperson of Guild For Services.

The fact that Jaya is a vegetarian from Kerala who has

been working in a completely alien culture in conflict areas like Kupwara, points to her dedication and determination to serve these poor children. People like Jaya give hope and a signal to people inside and outside the state that human compassion transcends the barriers of religion, caste, class or geographical boundaries.

Atiqa Bano was the founder of Meeras Mahal, a museum that was built in Sopore and which is a testimony to her passion for preserving Kashmiri culture and heritage. Atiqa was born in Sopore in an educated family in the 1940s. She graduated from Government College for Women, Srinagar, followed by a double MA in Economics and Urdu and Masters in Education from Banasthali Vidyapeeth, Rajasthan. She served in various capacities in the field of Education and finally became the Joint Director for School Education and Director Libraries and Research, Jammu and Kashmir in 1997.

Zaka Ur Rab M (Ref 39) reports that Atiqa set up an organisation called Majlis-e-Nisa in the seventies that worked for women's empowerment. However, she had a different and a bigger dream. She wanted to open a museum and that fire in the belly ignited her desire to collect old artifacts, coins, fossils dating back to Ashoka's time; manuscripts in Sharda script, Sanskrit, Persian and Arabic. She also preserved old copies of *Shiv Purana* and *Quran*. Collectables of the bygone era adorn her museum like kangris (clay pot with coals used for keeping warm and covered with wicker work), utensils, musical instruments, costumes from Ladakh and Kashmir, caps and jewellery used in everyday life of common people. She strongly felt the need of recording history and highlighting the unique Kashmiri culture and tradition and how important it is to keep it alive. In 2003, she started *Kashur Meeras*, a weekly

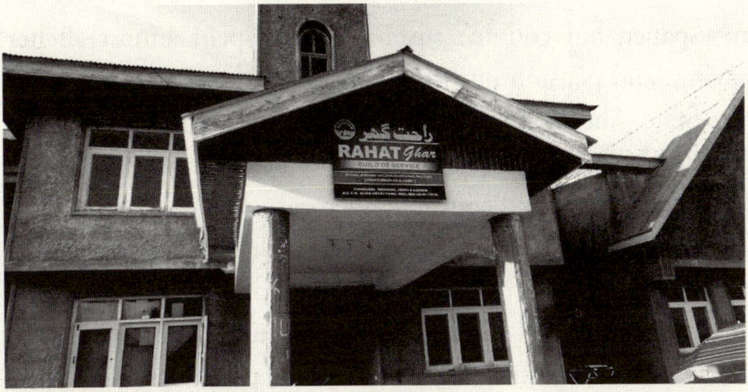

Rahat Ghar, Tangmarg (2018)

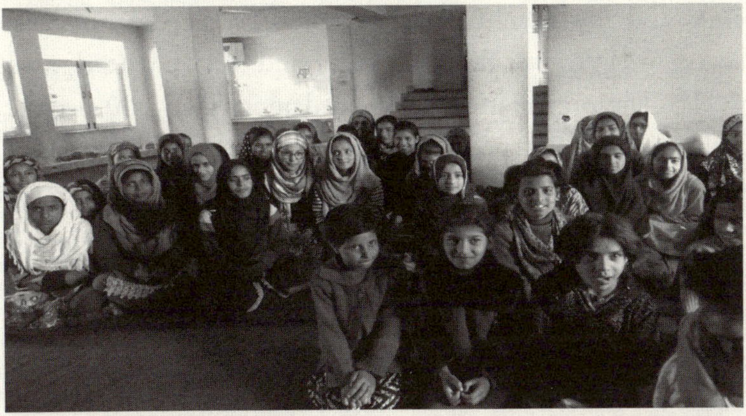

Girls (seniors and juniors), 2018

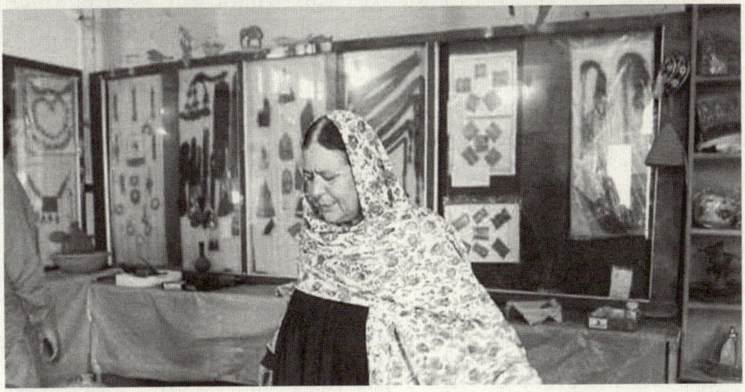

Atiqa Bano's museum

newspaper, but couldn't sustain it. She spent almost all her savings and pension on Meeras Mahal without any help from the State. She died on October 4 2017 but she continues to live in Meeras Mahal reminding every Kashmiri of the need to cherish, preserve and continue her legacy.

Athwaas Kashmir is headed by Sheikh Imran Bashir, and is an emergency relief organisation which came into existence on 7th September 2014, when torrential rains lashed Jammu & Kashmir causing massive havoc. Six lakh people were stranded in their houses, their property and belongings destroyed as cities and towns submerged in water. People did not have access to electricity, drinking water and food for nearly two weeks. The organisation has helped more than 500 people. Approximately 200 people were reported dead and floodwaters had also caused huge devastation to property, livestock as well as infrastructure (roads, bridges, hospitals, schools) with limited access to insurance.

Rescue operations were carried out by locals in makeshift rafts as state authorities were nowhere to be seen. Due to lack of boats, the majority of the stranded population was left to fend for themselves. SOS and distress calls made on Twitter once telephone and mobile services were cut off were filtered by their Bangalore Teams and then passed on to the Athwaas team at Srinagar via a functional telephone landline or WhatsApp. The team then rushed to rescue the people with the information provided to them over the phone. They managed to ship thirty tonnes of aid including lifesaving medicines, baby food, water, blankets, baby clothes etc.

The team members carried out rescue missions in boats and were out every day to rescue the stranded and vulnerable. One of the team members, Wasim Raja, participated in *Kaun*

Banega Crorepati in 2014 and won Rs 25 lakh on the show. Athwaas has also discussed the idea of setting up a primary healthcare hospital with the government authorities and is planning for free primary healthcare services in Srinagar. It will be the first hospital to run without any profit and will give free treatment, medicines and facilities to people of all communities.

Recently, Jaibeer Ahmed initiated a small endeavour called *Raabta* (a connection) to help find and reconnect old friends, neighbours, school mates, colleagues and families from Kashmir who had not heard from each other in the last 28 years. Using social media like Facebook (a separate page has been created) and WhatsApp, many Kashmiri Pandits and Muslims are reuniting and talking to each other, transforming hatred and bitterness into love, aiding the reconnection of two communities who have been alienated from each other all these years. A glance at the Facebook page is in itself a very emotional and a tearful experience indicating that despite the divide, Pandits and Muslims yearn for each other as they belong to the same soil and it is the bond with the soil that will always bring them back to Kashmir.

Meanka Handu is also attempting to bridge the divide through her comedy show on YouTube called *Asvun Koshur* (Smiling Kashmiri), a very popular show with more than 10,000 followers, viewed by Pandits and Muslims alike. This show has thawed the ice-cold vibes with undercurrents of distrust and hatred that the two communities nurtured for years against each other.

Yet another attempt has been made by Dr Amit Wanchoo, who launched an initiative called *Salaam Mahra*, a cultural and a social platform for the two communities to come together and renew old ties in April 2018.

Pragyna Wakhlu, a Delhi-based singer and musician is fusing Pandit and Muslim musical styles. In 2017, she released a musical album called *Kehwa Speaks*. *Kehwa* (local Kashmiri tea) is a metaphor for Kashmir. The saffron, cinnamon and cardamom allude to the oneness of all communities in Kashmir. She also uses other art forms like *Laddi Shah* (a satirical, humorous monologue on societal and political conditions of Kashmiri society) and *Vanvun* (sung during weddings by both Pandit and Muslim women) which are celebrations of holistic *kashmiriness*. She says, "Language is a common thread which binds us." Abha Hanjura is yet another popular singer who has transformed both children's songs and other Kashmiri songs into a modern genre of music. (Sarkar, Ref 29)

The case stories and contribution of some organisations and individuals described above is a small sample of a whole new wave of change makers that are rebuilding Kashmir. There are hundreds of men and women who are working silently to make a difference. I have not been able to meet all of them but their initiatives are critical to the rebuilding process. During militancy, parents were most concerned about their wards.

They worried about the future of their children in that climate of conflict and stress. Knowing that the gun culture would lead to their ruination, parents went to great lengths to put their wards in good schools. Vijay Dhar, Dilafroze Qazi, and Mrs Vijay and Pandita of Vasanta and Kashyapa Schools have made their contribution in producing a generation that can reason and counter the narrative spread by the separatists. This is a time when the provider (schools) and the receiver (students) have the same level of urgency to bring about 'normalisation' after decades of conflict.

Rehabilitators in the form of volunteer groups, civil society groups and NGOs are grappling with huge losses over the past two decades and trying to begin afresh. There are more than 200 NGOs working in the state. Despite the fact that some NGOs have been accused of siphoning funds and redirecting them for funding militant activities, many NGOs continue to do commendable work. Yateem Trust has provided succor to the burgeoning population of orphans in the past two decades. Guild For Services set up Rahat Ghar (now located in Tangmarg) which is providing residential facilities to children of single mothers in Kupwara and Zakura since 2000. Nighat Shafi has adopted a multi-pronged approach by addressing economic, social, educational and most importantly mental health concerns. Rahi Riyaz has been spreading health awareness and bridging the gap between service providers and the underprivileged communities.

Sajad Ahmed has given a boon to the children of his village by promoting martial arts while Nazir Benazir has been increasing awareness about environmental issues in the Valley. Other scions of culture like Atiqa Bano and Hasrat Gadda have showcased that Kashmir is not a conflict state but a seat of culture, art and literature. Gadda has demonstrated that 'the pen is mightier than the sword' by holding conclaves on poetry and literature at the peak of militancy. And our young generation like Jaibeer Ahmed and Amit Wanchoo are keen to reconnect and reconcile leaving behind a baggage of nearly thirty years of separation and pain between the two communities.

We can no longer afford to be isolated in a world that relies on cooperation, collaboration and mutuality through trade and economic ties. Interdependence and inclusion with secular and pluralistic traditions is the key to saving Kashmir and Kashmiri youth today. Irene Laure's words, (an indomitable figure in the French Resistance in post-World War II Europe) echo within me, '*Why are we ready to pay the price of war in lives and money and yet not pay the price of peace?*' For the love of our children and their tomorrows, should we not resolve our conflicts through peaceful means?

Mahjoor, the famous Kashmiri poet's words of hope and renewal, '*Vandchele, Sheen galiye, beye ye bahar' (winter will go away, snow will melt and spring will come again)* will surely be realised.

References

1. Andrew Whitehead (2013), Krishna Misri: *1947, a year of change*. Retrieved from http://www.andrewwhitehead.net/krishna-misri-1947-a-year-of-change.html
2. Athwas Kashmir. https://www.facebook.com/Athwaas-Kashmir-829025420461812
3. Bakshi, S (2009). *Kashmir; The History and Pandit Women's Struggle for Identity,* Vitasta Publishing Pvt Ltd, New Delhi
4. Bazaz PN (1959). *Daughters of the Vitasta: A History of Kashmiri Women from Early Times to The Present Day.* Gulshan Books, Srinagar
5. Handoo B (2017, September 28) Barkat's School. Kashmir Life. Retrieved fromhttps://kashmirlife.net/barkats-school-issue-26-vol-09-151831/
6. Centre for Distance Education Peace Education, Bharathidasan University, Tiruchirappalli. Retrieved from https://www.peaceinsight.org/conflicts/kashmir/peacebuilding-organisations/cdr/
7. Dabla BA (2016), A *Sociological study of Widows and Orphans in Kashmir*, Jay Kay Books, Kashmir

8. Devadas D (2017, December 8). Radical Land Reforms Were Key to Sheikh Abdullah's Towering Influence on Kashmir. *The Wire*.

9. Gupta A (2016, November 3). School burning: Turning the clock back in Kashmir. *Indo-Asian News Service*. Retrieved from http://www.india.com/news/india/school-burning-turning-the-clock-back-in-kashmir-1627477/)

10. Government of Jammu & Kashmir DOS (41)/17, *Digest of Statistics 2015-16*, Directorate of Economics & Statistics

11. Jehangir B (2017, October 16) *A history of health care in Kashmir*. JustjuKashmirnetwork.com/justju/? p=1070

12. Kashmir Tour Package. (2014). *Ancient Kashmir History*. Retrieved from www.kashmirtourpackage.org/history-of-kashmir.html

13. *Kashmir Reader*. https://kashmirreader.com/ Kashmir Times.com online edition, March 23rd 2014

14. *Kashmiris In Exile*. Retrieved from kashmiris-in-exile.blogspot.com

15. Kaul HN (1996, September). Kashyap Bandhu. *Koshur Samachar*.

16. Kaur R (1996). *Political awakening in Kashmir*. APH Publishing Corporation, Delhi

17. Mattoo N (2016, June 26). Down Memory Lane: From Widowhood to Women's Empowerment, *Greater Kashmir*

18. Mattoo N, Kashmiri Education. *Peace Kashmir.* Retrieved from http://www.peacekashmir.org/views-articles/2010/1009-kashmiri-education.htm

19. Médecins Sans Frontières (MSF), the University of Kashmir, Institute of Mental Health and Neurosciences (IMHANS). 2016. Muntazar: Kashmir Mental Health Survey Report 2015. MSF, New Delhi, India

20. Mirani H (2016, March 12). Agha Ashraf Ali: 94 and reading. *Kashmir Life.*

21. Mota A (2012, September 12). Kashyap Bandhu. *Chinar Shade*—Cultural and Literary write ups.

    Mota A (2014, May 23). Kashmir Sentinel. *Chinar Shade*–Cultural and Literary write ups.

    Mota A (2015, March 27). Fearless Krishna Misri from Kashmir. *Chinar Shade*—Cultural and Literary write ups.

22. Muju GK (2003). *Drops of Nectar.* Pandit Dinanath Muju Memorial Trust (Pvt), Jammu

23. Nayak A (2018, April 3). India's Failing Education System, *TheTimes of India*

24. Nehru PN (2012). *Satisar to Kashmir.* Naamu Publishing, Pune

25. Para HM (2017, December 15). Understanding Sheikh Mohammad Abdullah: Politics & Role. *South Asia Journal.*

26. Parimoo PLD (2012). *Kashmir and Sher-e-Kashmir—A Revolution Derailed.* Chinar Publishing, Ahmedabad

27. Parvaiz A, Dec 5 2012, *Conflict Kills Culture in Kashmir* Indian Press Service (IPS), Srinagar

28. Peer B (2004). *The school that helped build Kashmir.* Retrieved from *rediff.com.*

29. Sarkar S (2018, April 4) Bridge from Lost to Found. *The Telegraph*, online edition http://www.telegraphindia.com/india/bridge-from-lost-to-found/cid/1341224

30. Shamshad (2006). *A Sociological Study of the Kashmiri Women in Medical Profession.* Shodhganga—a reservoir of Indian thesis @inflibnet.

31. Sharma D & Rana A (2015). Social Evils Among Women In Jammu And Kashmir During Dogra Period And Colonialism

And Reforms 1846-1925. *IOSR Journal Of Humanities And Social Science (IOSR-JHSS), 20*(3), 8-20. Retrieved from www.iosrjournals.org

32. Sharma U (2014, March 23) Mehmuda Ali Shah: A Great Educationist. *Kashmir Times.com*

33. Scroll.in. (2017, December 14). *The Daily Brief.*

34. Sugra S (2017). Menace of Social Evils. *Kashmir Reader*

35. Tikoo T (2013). *Kashmir: Its Aborigines and Their Exodus.* Lancer Publishers,USA

36. Wanchoo A (2017, December 5). Remembering Wanchoo. *Greater Kashmir.* Retrieved from http://www.greaterkashmir.com/news/opinion/remembering-wanchoo/267957.html

37. Wikipedia, *Exodus of Kashmiri Hindus.* Retrieved from https://en.wikipedia.org/wiki/Exodus_of_Kashmiri_Hindus

38. Wikipedia, Vishwa Bharti Women's College, Srinagar. Retrieved from https://en.wikipedia.org/wiki/Vishwa_Bharti_Women%27s_College,_Srinagar

39. Zaka Ur Rab Mohammad. (2017, October 17) *Atiqa Bano, the lady who single handedly built a museum.* Kashmirink.in